# AIR FORCE MEMORIALS
# OF LINCOLNSHIRE

ROYAL AIR FORCE
WICKENBY
No.1 GROUP BOMBER COMMAND
1942 – 1945

IN MEMORY OF
ONE THOUSAND AND EIGHTY MEN
OF 12 & 626 SQUADRONS
WHO GAVE THEIR LIVES ON
OPERATIONS FROM THIS AIRFIELD
IN THE OFFENSIVE AGAINST GERMANY
AND THE LIBERATION
OF OCCUPIED EUROPE
Per ardua ad astra

## Midland Publishing
Limited

To
4128421
for all that there was,
and all that there might have been.

First published 1987 by Beckside Design
Reprinted 1987
Second edition 1988
Third edition 1990
Fourth edition 1995 published by
Midland Publishing Limited
24 The Hollow, Earl Shilton
Leicester, LE9 7NA
England

ISBN 1 85780 035 4

Printed in England by
The Alden Press
Oxford

Half title page illustration:
**Styles of memorial vary considerably and form
a constant source of debate. The Wickenby
memorial of 1981 includes a representation on
its face of Icarus, falling to earth.**

# AIR FORCE MEMORIALS
## *of Lincolnshire*

*Mike Ingham*

# FOREWORD

By Marshal of the Royal Air Force
Sir Michael Beetham GCB CBE DFC AFC DL FRAeS
Chief of the Air Staff, Royal Air Force
1977-1982

Ministry of Defence, Crown Copyright

Lincolnshire has a special place in the affections of most people in the Royal Air Force, and nowhere stronger than among those who served in the county in Bomber Command in the Second World War. The county was in the forefront of the bombing offensive and had more bomber airfields than any other. It was truly the 'Bomber County'.

The offensive was waged continuously against a wide range of targets throughout the whole period of the war from 1939 to 1945 and made a major and indispensable contribution to final victory. Night after night the armada of hundreds of bombers could be heard and seen taking off from airfields in the county and returning in the early hours. Sadly, a great number of brave airmen did not return and the many squadron memorials in the county commemorate their sacrifice.

In the following pages these memorials are recorded. This book serves both as an important contribution to the history of the dramatic events of the period and as an excellent guide for visiting the memorials.

*Michael Beetham*

Sir Michael Beetham
Marshal of the Royal Air Force
No 50 Squadron, RAF Skellingthorpe, 1943-44
No 57 Squadron, RAF East Kirkby, 1945

# PREFACE

Lincolnshire's links with military and naval aviation go back 80 years, and from one end of the county to the other there are memorials to squadrons and to the stations from which this flying took place. Although not all the stations and squadrons are yet commemorated by a memorial the list of those that are grows each year. Primarily they reflect the effort of the Second World War, but to set them in their unique perspective the events they commemorate have occurred within the span of a single lifetime.

Each of these memorials is more than just a record of a unit's history, for they represent a sum of individual loss. Those who were killed were the very ones each country could least afford to lose. Two underlying emotions may be experienced when visiting the memorials and burial plots – surprise at the obvious youth of those remembered and consideration of what might have been.

It is only right that we do remember, and not only the losses that these often simple yet moving stones and plaques are there to mark. The memorials cannot be an end in themselves, and are there as much for the present and the future as to commemorate the past. If we forget, we ignore. Our history is built upon the foundations of the past and we cannot ignore yesterday; it has shaped the present and is part of the future, and so we should recall those who went before – and learn the messages that have been left for us.

Despite the sorrow that these memorials must bring it is also fitting that the good that came from the evils of war should also be recognised. We should not only grieve for those who were lost, but also consider the good times too, and the comradeship and ideals that were forged amidst adversity. Flying itself has always been a great adventure, and so we should also remember 'Johnny Head-in-Air'.

This aspect of commemoration does not come easily, but the words of Pilot Officer John Gillespie Magee in his poem *High Flight* evoke the great exultation and freedom of flight. John Magee, a pilot on 412 Squadron Royal Canadian Air Force at Wellingore, was killed in a flying accident on 11th December 1941. He was 19 years old.

And so the reader is asked to pause, and to reflect on what the many memorials detailed in these pages mean. They are an important part of our history – a reminder to each of us of the true price of freedom – and also the responsibility that we all hold for the future. The task will never be an easy one, but we must work onwards together and so make the future worthy of the sacrifice of the past.

Mike Ingham
Lincoln, July 1995

# INTRODUCTION

The first edition of this book was published in 1987 as *A Guide to the Air Force Memorials of Lincolnshire*. It had 70 entries. This newly revised and enlarged edition has more than six times that number covering over 100 sites, together with details of other related aviation items. Many new memorials have been dedicated since the last edition, a number were previously unknown to the author, and other additions have resulted from a modest widening of the scope of the guide, which we hope will appeal to enthusiasts, historians and the ever increasing number of visitors to the county.

In the introduction to the third edition mild surprise was expressed at the continuing demand for a work of this kind, and the depth of interest in the field that it sought to cover. That there is now a fourth edition reconfirms that widespread attention, and reflects the number of new memorials which are being dedicated each year.

The original purpose went beyond the creation of a record of the commemoration in Lincolnshire to the men and women of the air forces. From the start it was intended to be a practical guide that could be used on journeys through 'Bomber County', as well as being a source of reference to those examining this specialised aspect of aviation history. These aims still apply.

Although Lincolnshire's links with military aviation began in the early years of the century it is the events of 50 years ago for which it is best known. Inevitably therefore this work becomes something of a record of Bomber Command.

As 'Bomber County' Lincolnshire was in the forefront of the Allied air offensive and stood at the western edge of the largest battlefield the world had ever seen, stretching almost 1,000 miles to the east. At its peak the county had more airfields than any other, primarily home to 1 Group and 5 Group of Bomber Command.

Almost half of Bomber Command's 19 Victoria Crosses were awarded to airmen operating from Lincolnshire. Despite the wielding of what was the most powerful weapon that this country had possessed – which played a decisive role in securing victory – it is a sad reflection on this country that no campaign star was ever issued to designate the effort and sacrifice of those involved. The effort was not only the acts of bravery of the aircrews, but also the sum of the many unhistoric deeds performed day in and day out to keep the aircraft flying. In reality the only permanent form of recognition is the memorials.

The story is not simply one of Bomber Command, and the county saw much other activity – day fighters, night fighters, anti-shipping strike, transport, and training activities also took place, together with less obvious aspects such as the work of the RAF's air-sea rescue launches. Airborne forces must not be overlooked, and a significant part of the Arnhem operation was mounted from Lincolnshire.

The RAF is unique amongst the nation's armed forces in that the fighting is carried out almost entirely by officers and NCOs. Even so, the contribution of each member of the Allied air forces was vital in its own way, from aircrew to the lowliest 'erk'. The RAF has built a strong tradition of teamwork and resourcefulness, and this extended in war to the strong links that were forged with the personnel of the Commonwealth and Allied nations.

The sheer scale of the logistics, organisation, and endeavour of this air offensive has never been appreciated fully, even amongst students of aviation history. If the scope of the county's contribution to victory is overlooked, the extent of the losses may be forgotten – another reason that this modest record exists.

History strides the landscape of Lincolnshire. A list of stations stirs the imagination, the names an echoing roll call of the past; Elsham Wolds, Hemswell, Scampton, Waddington, Cranwell, Coningsby, Metheringham, Ludford Magna, Binbrook, Digby, South Carlton amongst them.

Lincolnshire had 37 airfields in the Great War. At the end of the Second World War there were 49, more than any other county. The mean distance between each was only 7.5 miles, and a typical airfield took up over 600 acres. The total area occupied by airfields in 1945 was 29,000 acres – 2% of the county. Even today only 5% is occupied by towns and villages; 80% of the county is under cultivation.

This influence on the land was considerable, and rivalled the enclosures of earlier times. Its impact can be illustrated by a simple journey from Stamford north to Lincoln. Starting near to Wittering, the route follows Ermine Street into Rutland and back into Lincolnshire and passes North Luffenham, Woolfox Lodge, Cottesmore, North Witham, Spitalgate, Barkston Heath, Cranwell, Leadenham, Wellingore, Coleby Grange, Waddington, and Bracebridge Heath.

From the vantage point of the south west corner of what was RAF Hemswell the panorama of the airfield relates a story of Britain's aerial front line for three world wars. The remains of the former headquarters building of the RFC fighter airfield of Harpswell can still be made out at the edge of the cliff; the massive structures of the 'C' type hangars of RAF Hemswell's bombers sit in silence to the east, and in the centre the low bulk of the Thor missile wing bunker pays witness to a call that thankfully never came. But above all, the bulk of the wide sky dominates.

Lincolnshire's long association with the RAF continues, and nowhere in the United Kingdom is this association stronger. As well as its front line commitments, the county now has the distinction of selecting all officers and aircrew (at the Officers and Aircrew Selection Centre) and of carrying out the initial training of all officers (at the Royal Air Force College). Until the summer of 1993 the initial training of all other ranks was also carried out in Lincolnshire (at the School of Recruit Training, RAF Swinderby). The county is currently home to the Royal Air Force Central Flying School (CFS), the RAF Aerobatic Team, and to the Battle of Britain Memorial Flight. It also holds the distinction of being the only place where members of the armed forces are still trained in the use of crossbows (at the Aerial Erector School at RAF Digby).

RAF stations in the county are now Coningsby (air defence), Cranwell (RAF College and Central Flying School), Digby (signals), Scampton (Red Arrows), Waddington (airborne early warning and reconnaissance), and Woodhall Spa (engineering support). The relief landing ground at Barkston Heath now houses the Joint Elementary Flying Training School), and there are ranges at Donna Nook, Holbeach, and Wainfleet. The planned closure of RAF Scampton affects the CFS and the Red Arrows. Headquarters CFS moved to RAF Cranwell in May 1995 and the Red Arrows will move to RAF Marham in October 1995. However all is not entirely clear, and there are suggestions that the closure of RAF Scampton is not now definite. Among the suggestions is the transfer of two Harrier squadrons from Germany to Scampton.

The government's spending review of 1994 did not only encompass the use of stations. It was anticipated that an announcement would be made that the Battle of Britain Memorial Flight (BBMF) would be disbanded, to coincide with the 50th anniversary of VE-Day in 1995. Although regrettable, the sale of the Spitfire to fund the rebuilding of the Hurricane must be regarded as a positive sign for the future of BBMF, as is the very welcome decision to carry out the resparring of the BBMF Lancaster which is required at the end of the 1995 season.

For those wishing to learn more of Lincolnshire's inheritance, Terry Hancock's *Bomber County* and *Bomber County 2*, both published by Lincolnshire County Council, describe the development of military and naval aviation in the county up to the present day. The excellent *The Airfields of Lincolnshire since 1912* by Ron Blake, Mike Hodgson and Bill Taylor, produced by the publishers of this book, is the definitive work on the individual airfield histories. All three of these titles are out of print, but a revised edition of the latter is planned. Three other titles by Midland Publishing also extend reading on Lincolnshire – *Wings over Lincolnshire* by Peter Green, Mike Hodgson and Bill Taylor gives a pictorial record of flight in the county to the present day. Bill Taylor's *Battle of Britain Memorial Flight* provides a comprehensive insight into the history and operation of this Lincolnshire-based unit. *Aviation Museums of Great Britain* by Ken Ellis provides greater details of the museum locations in and around the county, as well as in the country at large. Details of these titles appear on page 72.

## Acknowledgements

Preparing a work of this kind has brought me in contact with very many people. I have been repeatedly grateful for the willing and helpful way they have all added to the overall story, giving freely of their time from often busy schedules. To each I extend my thanks.

It is hard (and not a little unfair) to single out individuals, but I wish to record my thanks to Marshal of the Royal Air Force Sir Michael Beetham for his foreword and for his long-standing personal interest in the book; to Mike Hodgson, Peter Green, Terry Hancock, Charles Parker, and Bill Taylor for sharing their encyclopaedic knowledge of Lincolnshire's aviation history; to Peter Green and Peter Wilson for advice and help with my photographs; to Terry Welbourn for designing the site map; to Cliff Smith, editor of the *Lincolnshire Echo*; and to Chris Salter and Ken Ellis of Midland Publishing for their backing for a fourth edition.

I would particularly like to note my appreciation of the support that I have received from Mike Hodgson, and of his enduring good humour and perceptive comments. I value greatly his friendship, and his considerable contribution to extending the knowledge of Lincolnshire's aviation history and heritage must not be underestimated.

All photographs are mine, except where indicated. It has not been practical to include a photograph of every individual item, but it is hoped that those published will provide a balanced example of the different types of memorial.

Finally, and not least, my thanks are due to Jackie and Tim. Above all for their unfailing patience (often sorely tried!), but also to Jackie for the original idea for a memorials guide and to Tim for his help on our many trips across this most beautiful of counties.

MJI

**Interior of the station church at RAF Digby.**

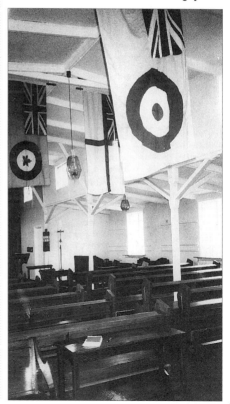

# HOW TO USE THIS BOOK

This book does not attempt to be a history of military and naval aviation in Lincolnshire – and in any case there are already outstanding works on the subject. What it does try to do is fill a gap in the overall story, by examining the history of that aviation from a particular vantage point and to observe something of the campaigns involved.

It is not simply an account of the Royal Air Force, but also its forebears the Royal Flying Corps and Royal Naval Air Service, as well as the links Lincolnshire has with the air forces of the Commonwealth and the United Kingdom's Allies (notably Poland and the United States of America).

Using a standard framework it lists those memorials to units – commands, groups, wings, stations, and squadrons – of the RAF and its forebears, and the Commonwealth and Allied Air Forces, in the boundaries of the historic county. Hence this is the *Air Force Memorials of Lincolnshire* rather than a guide to aviation memorials, aviation in the county being fundamentally military in nature.

Every member of the RAF and Commonwealth air forces who lost their life flying from Lincolnshire is, in accordance with the long standing policy of the Commonwealth War Graves Commission, commemorated by either an individual headstone over his grave or by name on the Air Forces Memorial at Runnymede. Those of the Allied air forces are similarly remembered, for example at the Polish Air Force Memorial at Northolt. Within Lincolnshire there are the memorial books in Lincoln Cathedral and the several squadron rolls of honour and books of remembrance.

For this edition it has been decided to maintain the principle of not recording individual graves. Apart from the sheer size of the task (900 individual graves would be involved), it would also be unjust to those others whose resting place is not inside the county's boundaries.

Unlike previous editions, there are entries for memorials to aircraft crews and to individual airmen, but in the case of the latter no detail of the inscription is shown. Details are given of the names on crew memorials, but not those in a roll of honour even (for example in the case of the 617 Squadron memorial at Woodhall Spa) if they are inscribed on the memorial. This has been not without much thought. Any distress caused by these decisions is regretted, and understanding sought.

There has been a broadening of what might be deemed to be a memorial. The wider subject of war memorials is touched upon in subsequent pages, and a more generous interpretation of the dividing line between memorial and commemorative item has been made. As before, there has been difficulty in categorising what may be considered as simply aeronautica. The authoritative definition of memorial in the *Oxford English Dictionary* – 'an object or custom etc, established in memory of an event or person(s)' – has been very much borne in mind, and it is hoped that a suitable balance has been struck.

Memorials to units of the airborne forces are also included; although these are to army personnel the association with the air forces warrants their inclusion.

There are entries for planned and proposed new memorials, although detail is limited to what is known at the time of writing. This also applies to locations, and in some cases only a general map reference for the site can be given.

The narrative is as comprehensive as possible and great care has been taken to ensure accuracy throughout. As before, any omissions or errors remaining are those of the author.

## Area Covered

The area covered is that of the traditional county of Lincolnshire which is set to be restored in 1996. References in the text to the county or to Lincolnshire are to this area, and not that within the present boundaries.

The recommendations of the Local Government Commission were accepted by Parliament in 1994. This will mean that for administrative purposes the existing (ie 1974) boundaries of Lincolnshire will remain, with two new unitary authorities replacing the southern part of the county of Humberside. The original boundaries of Lincolnshire will be restored for ceremonial purposes, although at the time of writing it is not clear how they will appear on future maps.

Two airfield sites which are partly in Lincolnshire have been included, even though the actual locations of the memorials themselves are not in the county. It has also been decided to refer to items which are just outside the county (within five miles) in view of their links with military aviation in Lincolnshire. Brief notes only are given of these, which are shown in a supplement at the end of the main text, and they have been included on the site map.

Lincolnshire's original size – 2,650 square miles – is often underappreciated, and it was England's second largest county until the local government reforms of the 1970s. Contrary to popular belief it is not flat (not all of it anyway) and it embraces a wide range of differing landscapes bounded on almost all sides by water; to the north the River Humber and to the east the North Sea and the Wash form the boundaries, to the west the River Trent traces half of the length of the county's boundary, and to the south the Rivers Nene and Welland mirror its general line.

From west to east the perspective shifts from the Trent valley to the limestone cliff, the central clay vale, the rolling chalk wolds, and the coastal strip with its marshes. To the south and east lie the fens, with their ruler straight roads and dykes. Above all is the vast dome of the sky –

the stage upon which were set the events that this work commemorates.

The airfields themselves, most now abandoned, stand silent witness to the people who built them and those who served on them. They form part of the landscape, from the mighty cathedrals of the 'C' type hangars to the crumbling concrete of former perimeter tracks and runways, poppies now touching the grass with colour.

### Sites and Locations

Memorials are listed initially by site (ie the place), and then by location at that site. Each memorial site appears in the main text in alphabetical order. Entries are listed by place name if a village site, or by the station name if on an airfield or other unit site. In the case of a disused station or airfield the service title is shown in brackets. Where there is more than one memorial at a site, they are listed under each location at that site. An index to units mentioned appears on page 71.

To reach most of the memorials it is virtually essential to have the use of a car. Like many rural areas Lincolnshire is not well favoured with substantial public transport services. Given the size of Lincolnshire it is unrealistic to expect that the majority of the memorials can be covered in a single weekend. From Goxhill (the most northerly) to Stamford (the most southerly) is almost 75 miles in a straight line. Thus a journey of 50 miles visiting only a few should be anticipated, and a round journey of over 100 miles in a day is not difficult to achieve.

### Maps and Grid References

In addition to the description of the site/location, each memorial has been given its Ordnance Survey Grid Reference (OSGR) number, and after a car the next requirement should be copies of the relevant Ordnance Survey (OS) maps. An appropriate street plan will be indispensable for Lincoln and the larger towns.

As well as helping to find individual memorials the OS maps also prove valuable in guiding the traveller from one to another in the most direct route, with the added benefit of seeing what is an unspoilt and very attractive county.

In some cases (for example the hospitals) the OSGR for the main entrance is given. This also applies to those memorials on operational RAF stations, where the OSGR of the main gate/guardroom for the particular station is given.

The OSGR uses the national grid system, based on a series of 100 kilometre squares overlaying the United Kingdom. These grids have a two letter code; those for Lincolnshire are SE, TA, SK, and TF. The squares are divided into smaller squares by vertical and horizontal grid lines. OS maps carry grid line overlays, and a six digit OSGR will get an accuracy down to a 100 metre square (strictly speaking at a point in the south west corner of that 100 metre square). The first three digits refer to the easting (ie the vertical grid lines) and the second three are the northing (ie the horizontal grid lines).

The most practical version is the 1:50,000 series maps (the Landranger series). Each sheet covers an area 25 miles square, at a scale of 1.25 inches to the mile, and gives detail on how to find and use OSGRs. Entries in this book show the OSGR prefixed by the Landranger sheet number and the letter code of the 100 kilometre square. For example, the entry for Lincoln Cathedral is 121/SK978718.

This translates as –

| Landranger sheet | 121 |
|---|---|
| 100 km square | SK |
| easting | 978 |
| northing | 718. |

Most of Lincolnshire is covered by sheets 112, 113, 121, 122, 130, and 131, with Stamford on 141, and the memorials feature on these sheets.

**Over 900 air force graves in the county and all have a story to tell. The gateway through to the burial ground at Scopwick.**

For absolute minutiae the 1:25,000 Pathfinder series is available, but it is not a really practical map for visiting the memorials. Its 2.5 inches to the mile scale gives superb detail, but almost 50 sheets cover the county. Lincoln is centred on sheets 764 and 781.

For general route planning the 1:250,000 Routemaster series is extremely useful, at a scale of 0.25 inches to the mile. Sheet 6 (East Midlands & Yorkshire) incorporates Lincolnshire, a small key map showing the Landranger sheets covering the county. It also includes the OS grid overlay and in most cases is an acceptable alternative to the 1:50,000 maps.

## Access

The locations of the memorials fall into four main groups –

> Those in public places.
> Those in churches.

Those on operational RAF stations.

Those on private property, or otherwise not readily accessible.

In the main, those in public places normally cause little or no difficulty to visit.

Those in churches may not always be easily accessible. It is an unfortunate necessity for churches to be secured more often, but the key is usually available close by (although details of the key holder are not always shown in the church porch). This may require some detective work, and the occasional return visit should be anticipated. When viewing these memorials the visitor will also find a rich historical inheritance awaits them. Lincolnshire's churches are part of our national heritage, representing one of the finest collections of medieval buildings in the country. It is believed that there are more churches per head of population in Lincolnshire than anywhere else in the United Kingdom.

There is no public access to those memorials on operational RAF stations. These can only be visited by prior arrangement, and a note of this is made in the main text. This cannot be over-stressed; operational and security demands remain paramount and an unannounced arrival will be met with a polite but firm refusal. Even a formal request may well be turned down, and access to some memorials may only be granted to those with a genuine reason other than curiosity.

Similarly, those on private property should only be visited if permission has been obtained in advance. Simple courtesy alone dictates this and, like RAF stations, in the case of some sites organisational factors have also to be taken into account and requests may be turned down.

A small number of commemorative items are not available for viewing at all, and the privacy of these items must be respected.

Contact details have been deliberately omitted, for two reasons. The first is practical, as custodians of memorials, responsible departments, church key holders, other officials, addresses, and telephone numbers are all subject to change. Secondly, it is only reasonable to avoid causing undue disruption which may be precipitated by the inclusion of items in this book.

Where there is a roll of honour in the form of a book this is usually held in some form of cabinet. This may be locked; quite apart from security considerations they will deteriorate through handling. Many locations have a copy which can be examined.

## Airfield Heritage Trails

The natural base for touring the county is Lincoln, and the local Tourist Information Centres (TICs) can provide information on accommodation to those wishing to spend some time in Lincolnshire. The visitor can also be helped by the innovative work of the tourism units of the local councils, and a joint leaflet has been produced by the County Council, North Kesteven, East and West Lindsey District Councils, and Lincoln City Council, outlining Lincolnshire's aviation heritage. Copies are available from TICs.

**The pioneering North Kesteven District Council Airfield Trail is marked with a series of panels, each using the appropriate roundel for RFC or RAF airfields.**

Notably, the work of North Kesteven District Council has produced the informative *Lincolnshire Airfield Trail* booklet, covering the area immediately to the south of Lincoln and eleven airfields. This trail is believed to be the first of its kind in the country, and in 1994 received an award from the East Midlands Tourist Board. Marker panels – with the correct roundel for the relevant period – identify former airfields. These are being supplemented by information boards showing a site plan of the particular airfield, and a map and details of the trail. Details are also in some cases displayed in nearby public houses.

The Airfield Trail is designed primarily for visitors travelling by car, and can be started at any point. The council has also produced a leaflet for group visits, including places of interest, hotels, and suggested itineraries, and also organises heritage weekends. Some indication of the size of the interest may be judged from the 50,000 copies of the booklet which were circulated in the first five years since it appeared in 1988. A revised edition was published in 1993, and again at the end of 1994.

West Lindsey District Council has also published its own *Aviation Heritage* booklet, a similar guide to the area north of Lincoln. Plans are in hand to extend the service in the future with a form of marker board, and two leaflets describing the aviation heritage and the various memorials in the council's district were published in the spring of 1995. It is also anticipated that East Lindsey may produce something similar in the future.

## Museums

Lincolnshire has a number of established aviation museums, complemented by a growing number of heritage/visitor centres. The main museums in the county – the Battle of Britain Memorial Flight, the Lincolnshire Aviation Heritage Centre, and the Bomber County Aviation Museum – are supplemented by the Newark Air Museum. Details of the museums are listed in the main text. They make an interesting and valuable addition to any tour, and enable a further insight to be gained into the scope and organisation of the Allied air forces in Lincolnshire. Each is well worth a visit, but as opening arrangements might be subject to an occasional variation it may be prudent for prior contact to be made before any long journey, to confirm opening/viewing.

## Can this book be up to date?

The simple answer is probably no. This does not infer some admission of inefficiency, but is rather a recognition of the ever-changing situation. The very great interest being shown in the memorials runs parallel with a desire to erect new ones, and the era that we are passing through is observing many significant 50th anniversaries, from the Battle of Britain to Victory in Europe.

Reluctantly (although inevitably) the line had to be drawn to end the research for this edition, effectively being May 1995. Where new memorials are planned or proposed, details are those known at the time of writing. A brief 'Late Additions' section can be found on page 70.

The final decision on RAF Scampton is still unclear, but speculation about the future of the Battle of Britain Memorial Flight is now muted.

Other changes may affect existing memorials, even if it is simply further information becoming available.

Although many changes are of a permanent nature, others – for example plaques and certificates – may be moved temporarily for cleaning, be repositioned, or even put into storage. Change may have affected the record shown in this work since the site was last visited. If a long journey is planned specifically to view a particular memorial it would be wise to check beforehand. (The county's tourist information service will help here, see page 70.)

Despite the disclaimer, this work includes everything that has been revealed by research over a considerable period. However, the full record of all the memorials to individuals is still unclear, and it is not really known what further items may yet lie in churches and other locations in the county.

If any reader has details of any memorial or other commemorative item not included, information would be very much welcomed by the author, care of the publishers, Midland Publishing Limited (see page 2 for address).

### Publisher's Note

During research for this book, the author recorded the exact style of the inscription of each memorial (together with the occasional idiosyncratic spelling or grammar which appear). Although the content of the text is reproduced here it has not been possible to follow exactly the presentations as they actually appear on the memorials, or to include every inscription. In order to present this work in a functional format, and within reasonable overall limits of space, the inscriptions have been typeset and laid out in a standard italicised style. It is hoped that reasons for this decision will be understood, which does not detract from this fine piece of research.

**More and more of the county's memorials are to be featured on road signs...others require more 'sleuthing'.**

# REMEMBRANCE

## The War Memorial

The oldest war memorial in the United Kingdom is said to be the great east window in Gloucester Cathedral, commemorating the Battle of Crécy in 1346. The wish to remember through some form of monument goes back centuries, a particularly fitting example being the Scottish tradition of erecting a cairn as a mark of respect for a fallen laird. The individual contribution to the memorial is noted in the Gaelic expression 'I shall put a stone to your cairn'.

It was following the Great War that the greatest construction of war memorials took place. (It was after all hoped to be 'The War to end all Wars'). They are to be found in towns and vil-

**The cenotaph at Grimsby.**

lages across the country and represent the greatest number of all public monuments. They are all around us if we should but look.

In those towns and villages they constitute part of the fabric of the community, inconspicuous by their familiarity. In style they range from the grand to the simple. Unlike the victorious monuments of more ancient wars these, for probably the first time, marked sacrifice and loss. Their purpose was not simply that of paying respect to the dead, but also to serve as a commemoration – and perhaps a warning – to future generations.

Often villages had a simple stone cross erected on the village green, whilst there are many examples of a statue of the figure of a soldier. An excellent example of the latter may be seen at Welton, near Lincoln, by the village church. The figure stands on a stone pillar, with names from the Great War inscribed on the main part of the memorial, and names from the Second World War inscribed on the base.

A further function of some memorials was to be of some practical use, although the original intention might later have become obscured. These ranged from memorial hospitals, village memorial halls, to public clocks and clock towers. One major proposition, the creation of an Empire war memorial involving a memorial shrine, bridge, avenue and buildings in London, was never realised. The Cenotaph in Whitehall – the symbolic empty tomb, designed by Sir Edwin Lutyens and dedicated in 1920 – stands as a simple, and yet more eloquent, national war memorial.

By comparison there were few similar local memorials set up after the Second World War, and village and town war memorials often had an extra panel inscribed to record the losses of the new war. Perhaps at that time the desire to build a better society was considered to be the finest form of memorial to those who had been

killed in the fight for freedom. By far the greatest number of memorials for the Second World War are those commemorating personnel of the air forces, with dedication of new memorials continuing to the present day.

Mention must be made of the superb work carried out by the craftsmen of Leake's Masonry in Louth. The company – founded in 1920 – has produced a range of memorials, from stone tablets to the might of 617 Squadron's breached dam in Woodhall Spa, and the design of what may now be considered the standard memorial stone across the county was created by Leake's. The first was erected 30 years ago at Kelstern to commemorate 625 Squadron, and the simple yet powerful style is also established as a pattern for similar memorials elsewhere in the United Kingdom.

A different but constant war memorial is to be found in the acts of remembrance that take place each year. These are a recognition and acknowledgement of all those who took part. Remembrance Sunday grew from the Armistice Day observance that followed the Great War. This was supplemented by remembrance of the Second World War and other more recent conflicts, and the focus of the nation's commemoration is the Cenotaph each November. Locally, Remembrance Sunday is observed in a variety of settings, from the formality of the annual service in Lincoln Cathedral to simple ceremonies by village war memorials.

These forms of remembrance combine with the wearing of poppies and by the annual Royal British Legion Festival of Remembrance at the Royal Albert Hall. The poppy is a poignant symbol which is worn with pride by so many of all ages, and the tradition was introduced in 1921. It has its origin in the poem *In Flanders' Fields* by Colonel John McCrae, a Canadian surgeon who wrote the words in 1915. Today 40 million poppies are produced each year.

Services held on Battle of Britain Sunday are services of thanksgiving, and not only services of remembrance. They recall example and fortitude, and confirm to members of the present day Royal Air Force, Royal Auxiliary Air Force, and Royal Air Force Volunteer Reserve that they are of the same company as those who took part in that most famous of endeavours.

The strong tradition of service in this country may be shown by the way in which many can identify with one of the companies present at the roll call at the Festival of Remembrance, and may point the way towards a possible future form of national remembrance.

Whatever happens in the future, the basic intention remains. All war memorials, whether large or small, commemorate the deaths of individuals. Their style, whether simple or imposing, does not detract from this purpose. We that pass by should do so with our senses open to their meaning, and respect those who gave their today for our tomorrow.

What of the memorials to personnel of the air forces? These new memorials may be compared to the established village war memorials. The names on the latter are those of villagers, and the former represent citizens of a different type of village.

Yet, on careful reflection another dimension might now be present with some of these new memorials, which may not have been intended with those established for many years. They are of course a mark of respect to former comrades. Perhaps they do more, and in marking the events those that are left somehow ensure that they leave something behind them to show that once they too were there — in a way a mourning of all lost youth.

As the echoes fade, the words on the 166 Squadron memorial in Kirmington village come to mind:

*Ye that live mid England's pastures green*
*Think on us, and what might have been...*

## Future Remembrance

Both world wars touched on everyone in this country; not only were there the casualties from the armed forces but also the many civilians killed or injured. For the first time civilians were in the front line, and the armed forces were in reality civilians in uniform; ordinary people in extraordinary circumstances.

With the 75th anniversary of the end of the first world war and the 50th anniversary of the end of the second there has been much discussion on the form commemoration should now take.

Quiet but insistent comment is made, suggesting that remembrance (and particularly national remembrance) should be discontinued as it is no longer appropriate either to the times or to our place in Europe. Parallels are drawn to our commemoration (or lack of it) of events of previous centuries.

Much of the doubt comes from a genuine wish to prevent remembrance becoming a ceremony devoid of real meaning. Sadly some of the debate has been insensitive, and the substance obscured. The key issues merit examination.

What exactly is being remembered, and who is remembering?

Despite the many wars, conflicts and 'emergencies' that the United Kingdom has been involved in over the last five decades, 'The War' usually means that of 1939-45. This is reflected in the number of air force memorials in Lincolnshire which mark the sacrifice of that conflict, but the sacrifice in all wars should not be ignored.

In an almost incomprehensible paradox, the ultimate purpose of war is peace. Recognition of all the principal aspects and the consequences of the course of events is not always easy, even at a distance. In many ways Europe has still to come to terms with its past, and it is also worth remembering not only what it was people were fighting *for*, but what it was they were fighting *against*.

Almost unnoticed, the personal links with the sacrifice of the past are being lost, but although the perspective may change all of us remain bound to the events of the past as they are part of a common history.

Remembrance encompasses many perspectives. For some the horror of war is not yet reduced to mere history, for others memories are eased with the passing of the years. For

**MRAF Sir Michael Beetham at the dedication of the 50 and 61 Squadrons' memorial on 3rd June 1989.** Lincolnshire Echo

some there is remembrance of close relatives lost, others (then only children) may have recollections of the adventure of the times, but for many it all occurred in the distant past and is only read about in books – or even not known about at all.

What, or who, is the remembrance for?

Is it an official form of remembrance, a reminder to us of the today given for our tomorrow, a message for the future, a sense of reaffirmation of belonging and faith in our society, or simply a remembrance by those who were there to respect those who did not get back? This will determine what form the remembrance should take and who should organise it.

By whose standards should we then judge what forms of remembrance there should be?

Should we be using as standards the popular opinion of the time (either then or now) with what might be differing approaches to the concept of duty, those of politicians who seek compromise and resolution (but who as a class do not always enjoy the unreserved respect of ex-service personnel), those of the journalist or armchair moralist, those of relatives, or of those who were there at the time – citizens of occupied countries and the many men and women of the armed forces (of the distinguished band like those of Bomber Command, who were described with affection by their Air Officer Commanding in Chief as his 'old lags').

This affects future air force memorials, which has already been influenced by a Ministry of Defence (MoD) policy decision, details of which were issued in March 1990. The MoD now discourages the erection of memorials on RAF establishments, in service churches, or on other MoD property. The understandable reasoning behind this move is the problems which might occur following a subsequent change of use.

The policy also reflects an official view that appropriate steps have already been taken to preserve the memory of those who gave their lives in the service of the nation. The policy document lists examples of these, including the memorial books in Lincoln Cathedral. The view is also taken that limited charitable funds should be applied for the benefit of those who suffered, or their dependants.

However logical this position, it should be seen against a very strong desire on the part of individuals and groups to commemorate those momentous events of the not so distant past. Although the MoD view can be understood, it seems to have blurred the very real distinction between official commemoration and what is the much more personal remembrance of those who were there. The number of official (that is central government) memorials in Lincolnshire is very small. By far the greatest number come from local initiatives and those of squadron associations.

In late 1994 the government announced its intention to mark the 50th anniversary of the end of the Second World War. Activities were to be concentrated on two periods; in May 1995 for VE-Day and in August 1995 for VJ-Day. In May the theme of official events would be one of reconciliation, celebration of 50 years of peace in Europe, and of hope for the future. August would be a more solemn occasion, commemorating the end of the war, and emphasising the sacrifice and achievements of the nations of the Commonwealth.

In the remembrance today, the wishes of the generations who were there should be paramount in any form of observance of the past. During the events marking the 50th anniversary of the Allied landings in Normandy the term 'veterans' gained common currency, adding (and

**Memorial to 625 Squadron at Kelstern, dedicated on 25th October 1964. A simple yet powerful style, this was the first of many aviation memorials carried out by the craftsmen of Leake's Masonry of Louth and now known as the 'Leake's Standard'.**

in no way detracting from) the respect given to ex-service men and women. The depth of comradeship, respect, and pride was demonstrated powerfully in the simple parade held on the beach at Arromanches on 6th June 1994. Despite its formal nature and its sense of history, the mood of the many thousands who lined up and marched past was clearly one of a family gathering, and the loyalty and respect for the Royal Family were unmistakable.

What then should the future remembrance be?

Should national remembrance make a sensitive and gradually evolutionary change, leaving local remembrance to its particular and personal associations?

National observance might build on the existing Remembrance Sunday ceremony, but move towards its very essence of service and sacrifice. Its general scope could be widened to remember all those who have given their lives in the service of others. The day might become a National Remembrance Day, dedicated to service to the nation (perhaps complemented by separate National Day celebrating our national heritage).

Such a change must pre-suppose not only an absence of war, but also the possibility of future wars. Events of recent years point to the reality which denies this optimism. Therefore if the message – and the lessons – of the past are to be learned by the young the remembrance of sacrifice in war must still play the fundamental and underlying part, and serve as a permanent reminder.

At an individual level the position of the Commonwealth War Graves Commission is a fine example; it makes no judgement. We should recognise the difference in others and build what bridges we can. A quiet dignity is fitting, and let us each remember and honour in his own way. Above all we should not forget our past.

As to Lincolnshire, it has been suggested that every airfield should have some form of memorial, so marking its place in history. Why should this not be so, and what better way than the standard commemorative stone that was created in Lincolnshire itself.

## High Flight

*Oh! I have slipped the surly bonds of Earth*
*And danced the skies on laughter-silvered wings;*
*Sunward I've climbed, and joined the tumbling mirth*
*of sun-split clouds, – and done a hundred things*
*You have not dreamed of – wheeled and soared and swung*
*High in the sunlit silence. Hov'ring there,*
*I've chased the shouting wind along, and flung*
*My eager craft through footless halls of air....*

*Up, up the long, delirious, burning blue,*
*I've topped the wind-swept heights with easy grace*
*Where never lark, or even eagle flew -*
*And, while with silent, lifting mind I've trod*
*The high untrespassed sanctity of space,*
*Put out my hand, and touched the face of God.*

*Pilot Officer John Gillespie Magee,*
*412 Squadron, Royal Canadian Air Force*

**The grave of poet and pilot J G Magee, in the village burial ground at Scopwick.**

## MEMORIAL SITES INDEX

**BBMF Lancaster PA474 in the colours of 9 Squadron.** BBMF

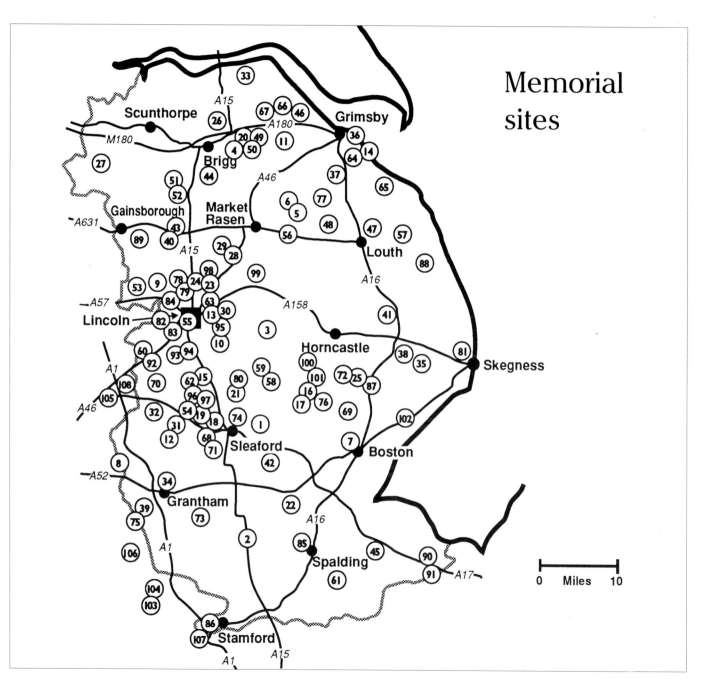

Memorial sites

# THE MEMORIALS

## ANWICK (RFC)     121/TF109519

On an unclassified road, east of Ruskington and north of the A153, is a **marker panel**, one of those placed by North Kesteven District Council for its Airfield Trail. The former landing ground nearby was used during the Great War. Carrying an RFC roundel, the panels reads: 'Former Anwick RFC landing ground'.

## ASLACKBY     130/TF088303

In the **village cemetery**, by the A15, is a **stone tablet**, set on a stone pillar. Below the inscriptions on the left is the Pegasus badge of the 1st Airborne Division. The front of the base notes that the memorial was erected by the Aslackby and Laughton Parish Council, supported by the Bourne branch of the Royal British Legion, United States members of the 29th and 47th Troop Carrier Squadron Associations, South Kesteven District Council, comrades who served in the Anglo-American Airborne Army, their relatives, friends, and local parishioners. The Memorial was dedicated on 9th July 1994, and carries the inscriptions:

*In memory of the American and British parachute and gliderborne troops, pilots and aircrew, who flew from the Aslackby & Folkingham airfield, and others nearby, to the European and North African battlefields in World War II, 1939-45*

*Their names liveth for evermore*

*British 1st Airborne Division
1st and 4th Parachute Brigade ('Red Berets')*

*United States 17th, 82nd and 101st Airborne Divisions*

*United States 52nd Wing, 313th Troop Carrier Group – 29th, 47th, 48th and 49th Squadrons*

## BARDNEY     121/TF120696

On the **village green** (at the junction of the B1190 and B1202) is a **three-bladed propeller** and spinner mounted on a brick base, and plaque with the badge of 9 Squadron. On the base is a stone from Norway, recalling the role of the Norwegian resistance in the unit's attack on the German warship *Tirpitz*. The stone bears a **plaque** with the inscription – *Scorpion Kåfjord*. The memorial was dedicated on 19th October 1980, and in late 1992 was moved a short distance to its current position. The small 9 Squad-ron room housed in the adjacent building has now closed, and most of the exhibits transferred to the Lincolnshire Aviation Heritage Centre at (RAF) East Kirkby. The plaque reads:

*IX Squadron RAF
In memory of all ranks killed or missing
1939-1945
The Squadron flew from Honington, Suffolk
1939-1942, Waddington 1942-1943,
& from Bardney 1943-1945*

## BIGBY     112/TA059075

In the **village church** (All Saints), on an unclassified road just off the A1084, is a **memorial plaque**, beneath the badge of 83 Squadron on the wall of the north aisle, with the RAF badge and the inscription:

*In loving memory of
Pilot Officer Harold Elvin Howsam of Bigby,
server and ringer in this church
and Flight Sergeant Gordon Fletcher
of London, Ontario
and of comrades lost with them on active
service with the Pathfinder Squadron RAF
on the night of 12-13th. June 1943
and laid to rest in the province of Friesland
in Holland*

*Grant unto them, O Lord, eternal rest*

**Bardney's 9 Squadron memorial includes a piece of stone from Kåfjord in Norway.**

Near the **village centre**, on the B1203 is a **memorial stone**, dedicated on 9th September 1973, with the badge and motto of 460 Squadron. A small plaque in front notes that the Squadron's roll of honour is in the village church. A **flower urn** carries the 460 badge. The inscription on the stone reads:

*460 Squadron*
*Royal Australian Air Force*

*'To those who served'*
*Breighton (Yorks)   Binbrook (Lincs)*
*from 15th November 1941*
*to 2nd October 1945*

*Strike and Return*

Outside the **village school**, (113/TF208942), on an unclassified road just off the B1203 is the upper portion of the **fin of an English Electric Lightning F.6** mounted on a base. The fin carries the markings of 5 Squadron (and the code letters 'AA') on the port side and the markings of 11 Squadron (and the code letters 'BA') on the starboard side. Nearby is a **plaque** with the inscription:

*Section of Lightning F Mk 6 tail fin*
*presented by the Commanding Officer*
*Group Captain John H Spencer afc raf,*
*and all personnel of*
*Royal Air Force Binbrook*
*to commemorate the end of the*
*Lightning era, and to mark the close*
*association between the Station and the*
*CE Primary School*
*19 June 1987*

Inside the school is the **pitot-static probe** from a Lightning mounted on a panel with the badges of 5 and 11 Squadrons. Nearby, a **plaque** carries similar wording to the tailfin above. Adjacent to the panel are framed prints of Lightning F.6 XS899 'AA' of 5 Squadron, and Lightning F.6 XR728 'BA' of 11 Squadron. Note that the items inside the school can only be viewed by prior arrangement.

Top: **Binbrook village school's Lightning fin.**
Bottom: **The 460 Squadron memorial.**

**In the village church** (SS Mary and Gabriel at 113/TF212939), on an unclassified road off the B1203. The **churchyard** contains a number of air force graves. In the **chapel of St Gabriel**, in the north aisle the **roll of honour** of 460 Squadron, held in a display cabinet and a 460 Squadron **badge** with the inscription 'In Remembrance'. In the cabinet with the roll of honour is the poem *To Absent Friends of 460 Squadron*. A **litany desk**, and plaque dated 9th June 1974 with the inscription 'In Memory of 460 Squadron RAAF'. A **stained glass window**, the Royal Air Force memorial window, was dedicated in 1988. The window displays the badge of RAF Binbrook and also depicts the RAF motto, details of squadrons stationed at Binbrook, a Lancaster and a Lightning, and the village church. The window has on it the inscription:

*To the glory of God and to*
*commemorate the life*
*and work of Royal Air Force*
*Binbrook 1940-1988*
*and in gratitude for the help*
*and support in the village*

A **memorial plaque**, dedicated to those on board Avro Lincoln II RF474 'PH-C' of 12 Squadron, with the inscription:

*In memory of the men of the*
*Royal Air Force Binbrook*
*who lost their lives in an aircraft accident*
*at Verquieres, France,*
*on 30th April 1948*
*on their return from the Middle East*

*Flying Officer Bernard Lincoln Lukins*
*Navigator Denis Godfrey Turner*
*Air Bomber Joseph Alfred Wise*
*Engineer Ernest James Gillman*
*Signaller Ralph Dear*
*Gunner Raymond Sleigh*
*Gunner Douglas Graham Brittain*
*Flight Sgt Frederick William Townsend*
*Sergeant Harry Sword*
*Aircraftsman Alfred Gilby*
*Aircraftsman John Hepplewhite*

The **standards** of 5 and 11 Squadrons. The 5 Squadron standard was laid up on 14th August 1983 and that of 11 Squadron on 19th August 1984. A **commemorative plaque**, recording both events, has the inscription:

*No 5 (F) Sqn standard laid up on*
*14th August 1983 by the Squadron Commander*
*Wing Commander M W Streten bsc*

A **plaque** in memory of Squadron Leader L H Glasspool, and of his daughter. The large **statue** of the Blessed Virgin Mary which stands by the entrance to the chancel came from the station Roman Catholic church when RAF Binbrook closed. Outside the south door is a **bench and plaque** in memory of Flying Officer H Pittard.

## BINBROOK (RAF)          113/TF199973

On the **former airfield**, adjoining a crash gate off an unclassified road west of the B1203, is a **tree and plaque** in memory of Senior Aircraftman A D Webb. Although close by the boundary fence, the tree and plaque are within the airfield boundary.

## BOSTON          131/TF327442

In the town centre, in the **parish church** (St Botolph), by the tower arch, at the west end of the nave is the **standard** of 29 Squadron, also an **RAF ensign**, and framed certificate with the inscription:

*On September 16th 1945*
*this flag was placed here as a token of the*
*affection of officers, NCOs and men of the*
*Royal Air Force who have been stationed in*
*Boston or at neighbouring aerodromes*

In the **municipal buildings** (131/TF325439) on West Street, is a **marble pen and ink stand** with Lancaster and Vulcan models, presented by RAF Coningsby to mark the granting of the freedom of the borough in May 1963. Part of the town regalia, it can only be viewed by prior arrangement and permission to view is not automatic.

## BOTTESFORD (RAF/USAAF)          130/SK821419

In the **former watch tower**, on an unclassified road north of Bottesford (between the A1 and the A52) is a **memorial plaque** with depictions of Lancasters, mounted beside the main staircase, with the inscription:

*1941 – RAF Station Bottesford – 1945*
*Dedicated to the memory of the men and*
*women of all nationalities who served with*
*the units based on this airfield during world*
*war two and of those who gave their lives*
*that freedom might prevail*
*No 207 Sqdn RAF Nov 1941 – Sep 1942*
*No 90 Sqdn RAF Nov 1942 – Dec 1942*
*No 467 Sqdn RAAF Nov 1942 – Nov 1943*
*US 9th AF Nov 1943 – Jul 1944*
*No 1668 HCU RAF Jul 1944 – Aug 1945*
*Their Names Live For Evermore*

Close by the plaque are the **badges** of 90, 207, and 467 Squadrons, 1668 Heavy Conversion Unit, the United States 9th Air Force, the joint badges of 463 Squadron and 467 Squadron, and **print** of a Douglas C-47 Skytrain of the 436th Troop Carrier Group and 440th Troop Carrier Group.

The boundaries of Lincolnshire, Nottinghamshire, and Leicestershire meet a short distance to the north of the former airfield. A major part of the former station site lies within Lincolnshire, although the tower itself is 100 yards inside Leicestershire. The building is now the head office of the Roseland Group. The memorial can only be viewed by prior arrangement, and permission is not automatic. See also 'Late Additions' on page 70.

## BRANSBY          121/SK899792

At the **Bransby Home of Rest for Horses**, signposted on an unclassified road between the A1500 and the B1241. The Home of Rest is open all year. Opening hours are 8am to 4pm daily. Admission free. Telephone 01472 788464. A **memorial plaque**, dedicated on 25th January 1992, mounted in a shelter in the picnic area, with a dedication to a 49 Squadron crew:

*In memory of the crew of a*
*Handley Page Hampden bomber*
*who lost their lives when the plane crashed*
*in this field after taking off from Scampton*
*RAF Station on 25th January 1942*

*Sgt Pilot Charles Duncan Stuart Stewart*
*Sgt Kenneth Edward Northrop*
*Sgt Albert Hibbet*
*Sgt Leonard Arthur Jardine*

## BRANSTON          121/TF031667

On **private land**, at the entrance of the drive to Longhills Hall (just off the B1188) is a **memorial plaque** to personnel of 250 Light Company Royal Army Service Corps killed at Arnhem.

## BROCKLESBY PARK          113/TA133113

In **parkland**, south of the B1210, can be found a **memorial plaque** fixed to a tree, marking the crash of Lancaster III ME442 'KM-V' of 44 Squadron. A new tree has been proposed, to be planted during 1995. Note that the memorial can only be viewed by prior arrangement, and permission is not automatic. The inscription reads:

*Wellingtonia Gigantea*

*This tree was struck by*
*Lancaster Mk III 442V*
*of Bomber Command RAF*
*shot down in flames by a Ju 188*
*on the night of 3/4 March 1945.*
*The entire crew of the Lancaster perished*

*This crew comprised*

*P/O J J Ryan – Pilot (Australia) – RC – Age 33*
*Sgt T H Jarman – F/Engineer – C of E – Age 19*
*F/Sgt R R Russell – Navigator – C of E – Age 21*
*F/Sgt H J Terry – Air Bomber – C of E – Age 21*
*Sgt H Birch – WOP/Air – C of E – Age 21*
*Sgt H Payne – Air Gunner – C of E – Age 27*
*Sgt W H Rogan – Air Gunner – C of E – Age 19*

*May They Rest in Peace*

## CAYTHORPE
130/SK939486

At the **village church** (St Vincent), on an unclassified road just off the A607. In the north aisle, a **plaque** commemorating the naming and dedication of the north aisle as The Arnhem Aisle on 15th September 1974. A **memorial plaque** dedicated to the personnel of the 1st Airborne Divisional Signals who did not return from the Arnhem operation in 1944. The **roll of honour** of the 1st Airborne Divisional Signals. A **memorial plaque**, dedicated to personnel of the 1st Airborne Divisional Signals who lost their lives in North Africa, Sicily, and Italy. A **memorial window** of three lights to personnel of the Airborne Signals. The window was dedicated in September 1994, to mark the 50th anniversary of the Arnhem operation.

Outside the church on the wall by the churchyard gate is a **memorial plaque** to the personnel of the 1st Airborne Divisional Signals and the villagers of Caythorpe.

Nearby, the **village war memorial** is modelled on the Commonwealth War Graves Commission cross of sacrifice.

**Cherry Willingham's village sign.**

## CHERRY WILLINGHAM
121/TF032727

On the **village green**, on an unclassified road south of the A158, the **village sign** incorporates an Avro Lancaster, reflecting the link with the former RAF Fiskerton nearby.

## CLEETHORPES
113/TA309086

In the **council offices**, signposted off the A1098. In the entrance hall of the building on Cambridge Street is the **roll of honour** of RAF North Coates. Two panels list the names of those killed on operations from the station in the Second World War. These were originally in North Cotes village church, and later in the station church at RAF North Coates. (Note the spelling differences of station and village.) They carry the inscription:

*Rest eternal*
*Grant unto them, O Lord,*
*and let light perpetual shine upon them*
*RIP*

The boards are flanked by the **badges** of 22, 53, 59, 143, 235, 236, 248, 254, 407, 608, and 812 Squadrons, the RAF Regiment (2705, 2802, 2854, and 2899 Squadrons), and 16 Group. The **badge** of RAF North Coates, which was presented to the Mayor and Corporation of the Borough of Cleethorpes by the station on 30th April 1959.

A **plaque** in memory of Sergent Chef (Fr) G Caron. **Portraits** of the Queen and the Duke of Edinburgh, and a plaque with the inscription:

*Her Majesty the Queen*
*HRH the Duke of Edinburgh*
*Presented to the Sergeants' Mess*
*Royal Air Force North Coates*
*by the Sergeants' Mess*
*Royal Air Force Binbrook*
*on 25 August 1988*

In the **cemetery** (113/TA299082), off Curzon Road and Mill Road south west of the town centre is a Commonwealth War Graves Commission **cross of sacrifice**. The cemetery contains a number of air force graves and a memorial to

**RAF North Coates roll of honour, now in the council offices at Cleethorpes.**

men of the Manchester Regiment, killed in an air raid on 1st April 1916.

In a **local church** (St Aidan at 113/TA293098), on Grimsby Road (A180) north west of the town centre is a **plaque** in memory of Flight Sergeant B H Cheer.

## COLEBY GRANGE (RAF)
121/TF011607

On the A15, just north of its junction with the B1202, at the **Boundary Cafe** in the car park is a **marker panel**, with an RAF roundel and the inscription: 'Former RAF Coleby Grange'. The panel was placed by North Kesteven District Council for its Airfield Trail.

Adjoining the panel is an information board with a site plan of the airfield, and a map and details of the trail. It is understood that a heritage/visitor room might be established in the future, possibly in the former watch tower (121/TF009608). Note that the watch tower is on private property, and it is not normally possible to visit the building.

**Easily visible from the A15, the watch tower at Coleby Grange provides an evocative reminder of the land's less peaceful past.**

In the cafe is a **commemorative certificate**, with the badge of 307 Squadron and the inscription:

*307 Nocny Dywizjon Mysliwski 'Lwowski'*
*Polskie Sily Powietrzne*

*307 Squadron of the Polish Air Force*
*operated de Havilland Mosquito NF XII night*
*fighters from*
*RAF Coleby Grange*
*during 1944*
*It was the only Polish Air Force Squadron to*
*be formed in Lincolnshire,*
*at Kirton in Lindsey in September 1940.*
*Amongst its original aircraft was the*
*Defiant fighter N1671*
*now on display in the RAF Museum at Hendon*

*Za nasza wolnosc i wasza*
*For our freedom and yours*

## CONINGSBY         122/TF223580

The **village church** (St Michael), is on the A153. In the **chapel** in the north aisle is a **memorial plaque**, with the badge of 83 Squadron and the inscription:

*This chapel was furnished by*
*members and friends of*
*No 83 Pathfinder Squadron and is*
*dedicated to the memory of*
*those airmen who lost their lives*
*on flying operations*
*from Royal Air Force Station Coningsby*
*in World War II*

As well as an **RAF Ensign**, there is a flag of the Netherlands, and a **memorial plaque** with the inscription:

*The flag of the Netherlands*
*hangs here to honour the memory of*
*Jacoba Maria Pulskens of Tilburg – Holland*
*who was a member of the resistance*
*movement during the enemy occupation of*
*her country in World War 2 her house being*
*used by Allied airmen in the escape network.*

*In July 1944, whilst housing three Allied airmen*
*F/Lt R A Walker dfc 83 Squadron RAF*
*F/O R E Carter 431 Squadron RCAF*
*F/O J S Knott (RAAF) 77 Squadron RAF*
*they were all captured by the enemy*
*and the three airmen were shot*

*Before being taken away herself and never to*
*return Coba Pulskens covered the bodies of*
*the airmen with the flag which now hangs in*
*this chapel as a tribute to her bravery and the*
*airmen she sought to protect*

Two **memorial plaques**, with the badge of 29 Squadron and the inscriptions:

*In memory of*
*Squadron Leader Stephen Glencorse RAF*
*'B' Flight Commander 29(F) Squadron*
*and his Navigator*
*Flight Lieutenant Graham Finch RAF*
*who lost their lives over the North Sea*
*on the night of 12th November 1980*

*Lovely and pleasant in their lives,*
*in their death they were not divided.*
*They were swifter than eagles,*
*they were stronger than lions.*

*In memory of*
*Flight Lieutenant A S Riley RAF and*
*Flight Lieutenant M R Hanton*
*Aircrew of No 29(F) Squadron*
*who lost their lives whilst flying*
*over the North Sea on*
*7th July 1982*

*'He hath raised us up together and made us*
*sit together in heavenly places in Christ Jesus'*

The **village cemetery** (122/TF222573) is near to the Battle of Britain Memorial Flight hangar, and contains a number of air force graves.

---

**RAF CONINGSBY**                        122/TF226574

RAF Coningsby is signposted on an unclassified road off the A153. Note that, with the exception of the Battle of Britain Memorial Flight, all the other items on the Station can only be viewed by prior arrangement, and permission is not automatic.

The **standards** of 29 Squadron and 56 Squadron. **Scrolls** recording the granting of the Freedom of Boston to RAF Coningsby on 16th May 1963 and the granting of the Freedom of the Borough of Tonbridge and Malling, Kent, to 29 Squadron on 28th April 1987.

**McDonnell Douglas Phantom FGR.2** XT891 'S' (9136M) is displayed by the main gate.

In the **station headquarters** building is the **roll of honour** 1939-45 of 50 and 61 Squadrons.

Within the cover is the badge of Bomber Command and the badges of the units. A **board** listing the Station honours and awards to personnel of 61, 83, 97, 106, and 617 Squadrons. An **engraved panel** with the badges of 83 Squadron and 97 Squadron, and showing Avro Lancaster 'OL-V' of 83 Squadron flying over the village church in Coningsby. Engraved on the covering glass panel is the inscription:

*Presented to Royal Airforce Station Coningsby*
*to commemorate the 50th anniversary*
*of the formation of the Pathfinder Force*
*on August 17th 1942*
*Both 83 (a founder member) and 97*
*Squadrons operated in that role from this*
*station from April 18th 1944 to victory*

**Framed certificate of 'adoption' of Lancaster PA474 by the City of Lincoln.**

In the **station church** (Church of the Holy Spirit) is a **memorial window**, The Japan Window, comprising an upper and lower light. The window was dedicated on 7th April 1990, in tribute to personnel of the British Commonwealth Occupation Force Japan. The panel records that it was donated and dedicated by members of the British Commonwealth Air Forces Japan Association. The upper light is a stained glass window of modern design, featuring a cross, gateway, and flowering cherry tree, with Mount Fuji in the background. On the lower light is a crown, and the titles 'RAF, RAAF, RIAF, RNZAF, PMRAFNS, WASB, WVS'. Between the two lights is an engraved panel with a **roll of honour**, the badge of British Commonwealth Forces and the inscription:

*1945-1952*
*British Commonwealth*
*Occupation Forces Japan*
*Yokohama War Cemetery*
*We honour those of our comrades*
*who died in Japan.*

Close by the window are embroidered **kneelers**, with the badges of British Commonwealth Forces, British Commonwealth Air Forces, the Royal Air Forces Association. A circular **stained glass window** above the altar depicts the dove of peace flying above the station and Tattershall Castle.

In the foyer of the **sergeants' mess** is the badge of 83 Squadron, presented in 1981. Mounted on a **carved wooden eagle**, it carries a plaque with the inscription:

*To honour members of this mess*
*who gave their lives whilst serving with*
*No 83 Pathfinder Squadron*

In the **officers' mess** is a **painting** of Avro Lancaster I R5497 'OF-Z' of 97 Squadron, dedicated to all who failed to return. Also a **painting** of a fox, carrying a plaque with the inscription –

*Presented to the officers mess*
*Royal Air Force Coningsby*
*by GEC Avionics Ltd*
*to mark the occasion of the reformation of*
*No 229 OCU 8th July 1985*

Also in the mess is an **engraving** of Tilburg in the Netherlands, presented to the station by the people of Tilburg at the 83 Squadron reunion in May 1983, and in conjunction with the memorial plaque in the village church.

The **Battle of Britain Memorial Flight** (BBMF) hangar and **Visitor Centre**, signposted off the A153. (122/TF220569). The BBMF was formed in July 1957 to commemorate the main battle honour of the RAF, and is regarded as a living memorial to both air and ground crews. Squadron codes carried by BBMF aircraft are changed at intervals — for example from 1994 the Lancaster carries the code letters of 9 Squadron. BBMF has the following aircraft on charge:

Avro Lancaster I PA474
de Havilland Devon C.2/2 VP981
DHC Chipmunk T.10 WK518
Douglas Dakota III ZA947
Hawker Hurricane IIC LF363
Hawker Hurricane IIC PZ865
Supermarine Spitfire IIA P7350
Supermarine Spitfire VB AB910
Supermarine Spitfire PR XIX PM631
Supermarine Spitfire PR XIX PS915

The Chipmunk and Dakota provide continuation training. The Dakota is also used for communications and as a groundcrew transport, as well as being available for display operations. This was particularly relevant during 1994, which marked the 50th anniversaries of the two major airborne forces operations, and the aircraft carries the markings of the Dakota flown by Flight Lieutenant D Lord who was awarded the Victoria Cross during the Arnhem operation. BBMF operated the Devon until the Dakota arrived in 1993, and at the time of writing it is still housed in the BBMF hangar.

Hurricane IIC LF363 was badly damaged in a fire following a forced landing at Wittering, Cambs, on 11th September 1991 and is being rebuilt by Historic Flying Ltd at Audley End, Essex. Completion is expected in 1996. On 26th November 1994 Spitfire XIX PS853 was auctioned to offset the costs of the rebuild. It was sold after the auction and delivered to the late Euan English at North Weald, Essex, on 17th February 1994. Supermarine Spitfire IX MK356 is under restoration to flying condition for BBMF at RAF St Athan, South Glamorgan.

Full details of the BBMF, past and present, appear in the book, *Battle of Britain Memorial Flight* by Bill Taylor. See page 72 for details.

The **Lancaster** has the **badge** of the Air Gunners' Association in the rear turret, being a memorial to all rear gunners. In November 1994 members of the Lincoln branch of the Parachute Regimental Association adopted the Dakota, which now carries the **badge** of the branch on the forward fuselage.

In the **BBMF headquarters** is a framed **certificate** with the arms and the seal of the City of Lincoln, dated 25th March 1975, and the inscription:

*Whereas during the years of the Second World War strong links were established between the citizens of Lincoln and the personnel of RAF Bomber Command by reason of the proximity of the City and many operational bases*
*And whereas one aircraft remains airworthy typifying the many which flew from Lincolnshire at that time and it is the wish of the citizens of Lincoln expressed most notably by the Lincolnshire Lancaster Appeal Committee that this long and continuing association be formally recognised*
*Now therefore the City of Lincoln acting by the Council of the said City hereby adopts Lancaster bomber PA474 bearing the name 'The City of Lincoln' and displaying the arms thereof: with the intent that so often as may be the said aircraft may be seen in the skies of Lincolnshire as a reminder to all of past efforts and sacrifices made in the cause of freedom*

The **Battle of Britain Memorial Flight Visitor Centre** is open all year – on weekdays only – and closed at weekends, bank holidays and for two weeks over the Christmas period. Opening hours are 10am to 5pm Monday to Friday. The centre is operated in conjunction with the County Council and embraces tours of the BBMF hangar (last hangar tour begins 3.30pm). There is an indoor exhibition, shop, refreshments, access and facilities for disabled people, toilets, free car park. Admission charge to the BBMF hangar. Telephone 01526 344041. Note - only those items available as part of the visitor centre tour can be viewed.

**Hurricane II PZ865 in the colours of 303 (Polish) Squadron as 'RF-U' (note the Polish insignia on the engine cowling) inside the BBMF hangar at RAF Coningsby.**

In the Visitor Centre is a **commemorative plaque**, with the badge of the BBMF and the Arms of Lincolnshire County Council and the inscription:

*Battle of Britain Memorial Flight*
*Visitor Facilities*
*Opened by Her Royal Highness*
*The Princess Margaret*
*Countess of Snowdon ci gcvo*
*30th June 1987*
*Royal Air Force*
*Lincolnshire County Council*

---

## CRANWELL          130/TF033499

At the **village church** (St Andrew), on the B1429, a Commonwealth War Graves Commission **cross of sacrifice** stands in the churchyard, which contains a number of air force (including RNAS) graves.

---

## RAF CRANWELL          130/TF008497

At RAF Cranwell and the RAF College (signposted on the B1429) are a wide diversity of memorial items. As well as those given here there are many other presentation items, but it might be difficult for them all to fall into the wide definition of memorial. Items held by the Central Flying School transferred to Cranwell with the move of the CFS headquarters, as part of the closure of RAF Scampton (see page 50).

A number of features, including College Hall, Queen's Avenue, the plaques commemorating the avenues of trees, and the gate guard can be seen (and the chime heard) from the public road. All the other items on the station can only be viewed by prior arrangement, and permission is not automatic.

Adjoining the gates of **College Hall** are two pillars, commemorating an avenue of trees behind. Nearby are many other trees planted over the years, each having a small plaque at its base. On each pillar is a **commemorative plaque**, one bearing the inscription 'Queen's Avenue'.

On the other is the inscription:

*This avenue*
*was opened on 25th July 1960 by*
*Her Majesty The Queen*
*It commemorates Her Majesty's gracious*
*assumption in April 1960 of the appointment*
*of Commandant-in-Chief and presentation in*
*July 1960 of a new colour to the*
*Royal Air Force College*

Mounted on the railings of the gates of College Hall are **commemorative plaques**. Both carry inscriptions, both with similar wordings, for either the eastern or western avenue of limes:

*This and the Eastern Avenue of lime trees*
*were presented by the Right Honourable*
*Sir Samuel Hoare, Bart, pc, gbe, cmg etc.*
*Secretary of State for Air 1922-24 & 1924-29*

**BAC Jet Provost T.5A** XW353 '3' (9090M) is displayed near the main gate. Two other aircraft displayed at RAF Cranwell are **McDonnell Douglas Phantom FGR.2** XV408 'Z' (9165M) displayed outside the Officers and Aircrew Selection Centre, and **English Electric Canberra B.2T** 'WH699' (actually WJ637/8755M) displayed outside Trenchard Hall.

The **College Church** (St Michael and All Angels) was dedicated on 1st June 1962, the Memorial Chapel being in the north aisle. The original Memorial Chapel (known as St Michael's Chapel) was in the west wing of the College building. It was dedicated on 22nd June 1952 to commemorate those former cadets who had lost their lives, from those trained before the Second World War. Their names are inscribed in a **memorial book**, displayed in a case which is inscribed with the 'theatres; in which lives were lost : Britain, Egypt, Atlantic, Palestine, Greece, Aden, Malta, India, Italy, Iraq, North Africa, South East Asia, North West Europe and the Far East. Another **memorial book**, displayed in a case carries the names of those former Flight Cadets and Graduate Entrant Officers who have lost their lives flying in the RAF since 1945. A further **memorial book**, displayed in a case carries the names of servicemen who are buried in the in Cranwell village churchyard.

**As might be imagined, the Royal Air Force College holds a wealth of memorial items.**

A **lectern**, with a roll of honour of Royal Naval Air Service and Royal Air Force personnel. The names are carved on the shelf of the lectern. The **King's Colour** for the Royal Air Force College, presented 6th July 1948. This was the first Sovereign's Colour presented to the RAF. The **Queen's Colour** for the Royal Air Force College, presented 21st July 1960 and the **Queen's Colour** for the Royal Air Force College, presented 30th May 1975. The colours are laid up in the church. The church also contains many **badges** mounted on pew ends, and a **book of donors** to the College Memorial Chapel. Outside is a **tree and plaque** in memory of Air Chief Marshal Sir Neville Stack.

In **College Hall** is the **Queen's Colour** for the Royal Air Force College. The Rotunda holds a number of **squadron standards**. These are temporarily lodged in the care of the College, and are not formally laid up. Recently the standards were those of 35, 44, 50, 58, 92, 99, 203, 204, 205, 209 and 210 Squadrons.

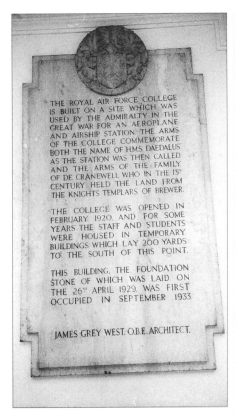

**Plaque detailing the background of the Cranwell site.**

The **College Chime** not only marks the hours but also sounds the *Retreat*, when the RAF Ensign and the College Flag are lowered each day. A **memorial plaque**, dated 1952, mounted inside the entrance to College Hall carries the inscription:

*This plaque cast in the metal of the bells*
*of the College Chime records the gratitude of*
*the College to the Shell Group through whose*
*generosity the Chime was presented as a*
*memorial to those old Cranwellians who have*
*given their lives in service of their country and*
*as a daily reminder of their gallantry and*
*sacrifice*

The **Battle of Britain Trophy**, awarded to the best aerobatic pilot on each entry, in the form of a crane (from the College arms) and presented by the Battle of Britain Fighter Association to commemorate 'The Few'. At the time it was first awarded in 1963 it was unique in being the only College award open to all three services. The **armorial bearings** of the College, the original bearings and those marking the 50th anniversary of the College. A **scroll** recording the granting of the Freedom of Sleaford to the College on 29th September 1991.

A large **commemorative plaque**, with the College arms and the name of the architect, James Grey West OBE. Below the plaque are the two volumes of **The Roll of the Royal Air Force College**, which records the names of all those cadets who have served on courses at the College. On the plaque is the inscription:

*The Royal Air Force College*
*is built on a site which was used by the*
*Admiralty in the Great War for an aeroplane*
*and airship station. The arms of the College*
*commemorate both the name of HMS*
*Daedalus as the Station was then called, and*
*the arms of the family de Cranewell who in*
*the 13th Century held the land from the*
*Knights Templars of Brewer.*
*The College was opened in February 1920,*
*and for some years the staff and students*
*were housed in temporary buildings which lay*
*200 yards to the south of this point. This*
*building, the foundation stone of which was*
*laid on the 26th April 1929, was first*
*occupied in September 1933.*

To the left of the main entrance door is the **foundation stone**, with the badge of the RAF. This stone was laid by the Lady Maud Hoare DBE on 26th April 1929. A **time capsule** was placed under the stone. To the right of the main entrance door is the **commemorative stone** marking the official opening of the College, by His Royal Highness The Prince of Wales KG on 11th October 1934.

Outside the **headquarters of the College Band** are two flowering cherry trees, dedicated in May 1986, and a **memorial plaque** dedicated to the memory of personnel of the RAF Germany Band who died in a road accident on 11th February 1985.

The names of two of the halls commemorate individuals — Trenchard Hall and Whittle Hall. Both buildings have appropriate foundation stones. To the rear of **Trenchard Hall** is a **memorial plaque** mounted on a brick pillar, with the badge of the RAF Electrical and Wireless School on the front and the badge of the RAF Technical College on the rear. The plaque reads:

*This plaque was erected*
*by the Cranwell Electrical & Wireless*
*School Boy Entrants Association*
*to commemorate the*
*Boy Entrants who trained here*
*between 1934-1940*

For further details of Cranwell college and airfield, past and present, see the companion volume, *Cranwell*: RNAS & RAF Photographs by Peter Green and Mike Hodgson – details on page 72.

Please note that the **RAF Cranwell Aviation Heritage Centre** is listed under the location heading of North Rauceby.

---

**CROXTON**      112/TA094122

The **village church** (St John), is just off the A1077. The **churchyard** contains the grave of Sergeant T I Dee, the private **headstone** depicting a navigator's flying badge and an Avro Lancaster. Inside, the **east window** has a memorial plaque with the badge of the RAF and the inscription:

*To the glory of God*
*and in perpetual remembrance of*
*Sergeant Navigator Timothy l'Anson Dee*
*RAFVR aged 20 years, who was killed with*
*four other members of the crew,*
*on December 16th 1943, when their plane*
*crashed near Linton-on-Ouse, Yorkshire*
*returning from operations over Berlin.*

*They gave their lives that we might live*

## RAF DIGBY

At RAF Digby (signposted on the B1191) by the main gate is a **memorial stone**, with the badges of the Royal Canadian Air Force and 411 Squadron. On the left and right faces of the pillar are the theatres of operation for the squadron : Defense of Britain 1941-44, Fortress Europe 1941-44, Dieppe, English Channel and North Sea 1942-43, Arnhem, France and Germany 1944-45, Normandy 1944 and the Rhine. The inscription on the front reads:

*This Canadian granite stone is placed on the occasion of the 50th anniversary of the formation of 411 Squadron Royal Canadian Air Force here at Royal Air Force Station Digby on 16th June 1941*

*This memorial is in memory of the dedication of all Squadron members who have served, and continue to serve Canada and the world*

*Inimicus Inimico*
*Hostile to an Enemy*

Replica **Supermarine Spitfire IX** 'MJ832' (BAPC.229) in the colours of 'DN-Y' of 416 Squadron and carrying the legend 'City of Oshawa' by the cockpit, is mounted on a plinth, and a **memorial plaque** carries the inscription:

*Spitfire Mk IX*
*This Spitfire is a replica of an aircraft flown by the Royal Canadian Air Force from RCAF Digby during the period 1942-1945*

*It was dedicated on the 75th anniversary of the Station to all personnel, service and civilian, who have served here at RAF Digby (previously known as RAF Scopwick and RCAF Digby) and also the former satellite airfields at Coleby Grange and Wellingore*

*The airfield was opened on 28 March 1918*

In the **station church** (SS Michael and Andrew) is an **RAF Ensign** and an **RCAF Ensign**. The church contains a range of other items, these include **stained glass windows** in the

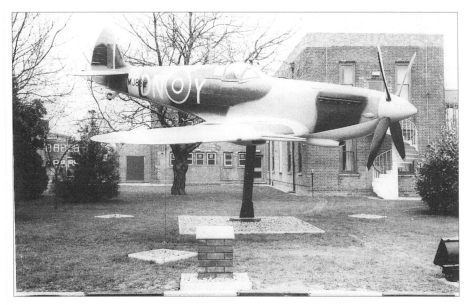

Full size replica Spitfire on the gate at RAF Digby, carrying the markings of 416 Squadron RCAF, which was based at Digby.

clerestory, showing the badges of RAF Digby, HMS *Daedalus*, the RAF, the RCAF, 12 Group, 90 Group, 399 Signals Unit and 591 Signals Unit, and a White Ensign. The church, which was rededicated on 7th June 1972, has pews from St George's church at Changi, Singapore. The original **station bell** is held in the **station headquarters** building.

## DONINGTON

At the **village church** (St Mary and the Holy Rood), between the A52 and the A152, is the **Arnhem Tree**, commemorating personnel of the airborne forces who were stationed in the area. In the **church** is a **commemorative plaque** presented on 25th September 1994 by the Airborne Engineers' Association.

It is understood that the **commemorative plaque** presented by the Ministry of Aircraft Production for Supermarine Spitfire V R7290 'Doningtonian' is now held in the Spalding area. However, it is not available for viewing.

Canadian granite honouring 411 Squadron RCAF, at RAF Digby.

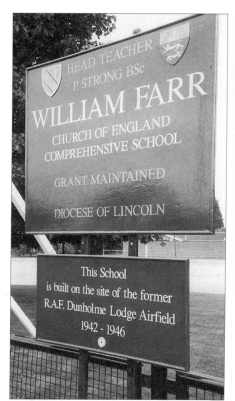

**The William Farr School is built on the domestic site of Dunholme Lodge and incorporates the original NAAFI building.**

## DUNHOLME 121/TF025794

In the **village church** (St Chad), on the A46, is a circular **memorial plaque**, dedicated on 21st May 1989, on the wall of the south aisle. In the churchyard is an air force grave. The circular plaque carries the badge of 44 Squadron and the inscription:

*44 (Rhodesia) Squadron Royal Air Force*
*In memory of those who served at*
*Royal Air Force Dunholme Lodge*
*May 1943 – Sept 1944*

*'We will remember them'*

## DUNHOLME LODGE (RAF) 121/TF012793

On an unclassified road between the A15 and the A46, the **William Farr School**, Welton, is built on the officers' mess and sergeants' mess domestic site of the former station, and incorporates the original NAAFI building. Although the exterior sign can be viewed from the roadside, the panel inside the hall and other items can only be viewed by prior arrangement, and permission is not automatic.

**Outside** the school is a **panel** mounted below the school name sign, with an RAF roundel and an inscription noting that the school is built on the site of the former airfield. In the **school hall** is a **display board**, with the badges of the RAF Aerobatic Team, the Red Arrows, the William Farr School, and an inscription noting the names of those gaining a High Flyers award for the best academic achievement at GCSE examination level and similar wording to the panel outside. In the **library** is a range of material relating to RAF Dunholme Lodge, including photographs of Polish Air Force and Polish Resettlement Corps personnel. A history of 619 Squadron has been presented to the school, and a permanent display is being considered. There is also a framed **certificate** noting the Station's usage: RAF 1942-46, Polish Air Force and Polish Resettlement Corps 1946-47 and RAF 1958-64.

## EAST KIRKBY (RAF/USAF) 122/TF337624

At the entrance to the **Lincolnshire Aviation Heritage Centre**, (signposted just off the A155) is a **memorial stone**, dedicated on 6th October 1979 on the site of the former guardroom. It features a Lancaster in plan form engraved at the top of the stone, which is surrounded by a low fence with a Lancaster depicted on the front and with the badges of 57 Squadron and 630 Squadron. By the stone is a **flower urn** in memory of Pilot Officer F W Logan RCAF and also a **flower box**, carrying the figures '57' and '630'. The inscription on the stone reads:

*In memory of those who gave their lives with*
*57 and 630 Squadrons*
*1939-1945*

On the left of the memorial stone is a **plaque** with the poem *Old Airfield*, written by a former member of 630 Squadron. On the right of the memorial stone is a **plaque** with the inscription:

*Members of 57 and 630 Squadrons who erected this memorial pay tribute to the people of East Kirkby who made them welcome in both war and the peace that followed and generously contributed to the memorial fund*
*This memorial stands on the site of the guard room of the airfield from which both squadrons operated between August 30th 1943 and April 25th 1945 and from which over 1,000 air crew 'went missing'*
*October 1979*

The Lincolnshire Aviation Heritage Centre is open all year, Monday to Saturday. Note that it is closed on Sundays. Opening hours are Easter to October 10am to 5pm (last admission 4pm) Monday to Saturday. November to Easter 10am to 4pm (last admission 3pm) Monday to Saturday. A wide range of display items is featured in a purpose-built hangar, the primary exhibit being the Avro Lancaster, and includes exhibits transferred from the 9 Squadron museum at Bardney. The centre also incorporates the former watch tower, an escaping exhibition, military vehicles, other special exhibitions, plus shop, refreshments, access and facilities for disabled people, toilets, free car park. Admission charge. Telephone 01790 763207.

In the **exhibition hangar** is a **memorial plaque**, with the inscription:

*Lincolnshire Aviation Heritage Centre*
*opened by*
*Marshal of the Royal Air Force Sir Michael Beetham gcb, cbe, dfc, afc*
*on 8th July 1989*
*as a memorial to Bomber Command*
*1939-1945*

A circular stained glass **memorial window**, with the badge of 617 Squadron also depicting an Avro Lancaster, de Havilland Mosquito, English Electric Canberra, Avro Vulcan, and Panavia Tornado, with the inscription:

*1943-55*
*1958-81*
*1983-93*
*To Commemorate the 50th anniversary of*
*617 Squadron The Dambusters*

Another **memorial plaque**, unveiled in April 1992 by the widow and son of Sergeant Rusby. It forms part of a **commemorative display** to the crew of the Armstrong Whitworth Albemarle, from 42 Operational Training Unit, shot down at Kirton Fen. The other two crew members parachuted to safety. The inscription reads:

*This display is dedicated to the memory of*
*Sgt J E Hutchinson (pilot)*
*Sgt K Rusby (navigator)*
*Sgt A A Whittome (bomb-aimer) RAF*
*who were killed in Albemarle V1610*
*on 23 April 1944*

A **commemorative scroll** to Sergeant K Rusby. A small **memorial plaque**, part of a display to the crew of the Lancaster, which crashed at Roughton Moor. The text at its head being the squadron motto, followed by:

*Corpus non animum muto*
*57 Sqn Lancaster W4250 10th Dec 1942*
*W/O₂ G H Ramey – P/O J F McPherson*
*P/O A J McLaughlin – Sgt R B Dion*
*Sgt K W Pharoah – F/Sgt T N McLeod*
*Sgt W O Lundy*

There is another circular stained glass **memorial window**, depicting scenes and figures connected with the attack on the Ruhr dams, including Wing Commander G P Gibson and his dog 'Nigger', Avro Lancasters, and Lincoln Cathedral. The inscription reads:

*16th May 1943 617 Squadron*
*To commemorate*
*the 50th anniversary of the Dams raid*
*17th May 1943*
*The Dambusters*

A **display** featuring items recovered from the crash site of B-24 Liberator 42-95103 of the 392nd Bombardment Group. A memorial plaque to the crew is in the village church, Wrangle (see entry). A **display** in memory of Kapral A Bardecki of 316 Squadron, who was killed on 2nd October 1944 when his North American Mustang crashed in Norfolk. The display includes the badge of 316 Squadron, and the Polish Air Force 'chequerboard' national marking.

**All of the Lincolnshire Aviation Heritage Centre is dedicated as a memorial to Bomber Command. At the main entrance is a memorial stone to the sacrifice of 57 and 630 Squadrons.**

The **gates** of RAF North Coates – with the letters 'RAF' and 'NC' fashioned in the wrought iron – and a **plaque** with the inscription:

*Royal Air Force Northcoates*
*main entrance gates*
*(circa pre 1940)*
*presented to the*
*Lincolnshire Aviation Heritage Centre*
*by RAF North Coates on its closure*
*November 1990*

The **badge** of Pensacola Naval Air Station, presented by the British Pensacola Veterans, 21st November 1988. Nearby is a proclamation from the mayor of the City of Pensacola to the British Pensacola Veterans Reunion 1986.

An **acrylic panel**, with the badge of the City of Pensacola, signed by the mayor and presented to the British Pensacola Veterans. Also framed **certificate**, dated 25th August 1986 and again signed by the mayor of Pensacola, with the inscription:

*City of Pensacola, Florida
Commendation*
*The City of Pensacola awards to the British
Pensacola Veterans this expression of grateful
acknowledgement for your valued services
rendered in the public interest for the
continued bond of friendship between the
United Kingdom and the USA and is
tendered with the sincere appreciation of your
fellow citizens*

**Avro Lancaster VII** NX611 in the colours of 57
Squadron as 'DX-C' 'Just Jane' on the starboard
side and 630 Squadron as 'LE-C' on the port side
is a Memorial to all Lancasters, to the aircrews
who flew them and to the groundcrews who
serviced them. The aircraft previously stood by
the main gate at RAF Scampton. NX611 is also a
memorial to Pilot Officer C W Panton, brother of
the owners of the airfield and museum, who
was lost his life flying on 433 Squadron, and who
is also commemorated by a tree in the garden
of remembrance outside the hangar.

The salvaged forward fuselage of Supermarine Spitfire Vb BL655 and a **plaque** in memory
of Norman Watt of 416 Squadron, killed whilst
flying the aircraft, 1st July 1943.

The hangar contains a comprehensive range
of station and squadron details, including panels with the **badges** of 11, 23, 56, 74, 92, and 111
Squadrons, and boards listing the station commanders of RAF Binbrook and RAF North
Coates, flying units stationed at RAF Binbrook,
and the movements and equipment of 68
Squadron, as well as items relating to units stationed at RAF East Kirkby.

**Outside the hangar** a **garden of remembrance** has been established, each tree having
a plaque at its base. Single **trees and plaques**
can be found in memory of Pilot Officer C W
Panton, another in memory of Warrant Officer J
Woodrow and another in memory of Flight
Sergeant Tomney. Three of the trees carry crew
memorial plaques, as follows:

*This tree commemorates the following crew
P/O F Collis, F/Sgt J Fox, F/O R Essery, Sgt J
Topple, F/Sgt J Griffith, F/Sgt J Skinner,
F/Sgt N Atkin – 207 Sqn 1943-1944*

**A pair of circular stained glass windows devoted to aspects of 617 Squadron can be found among the displays at East Kirkby.**

*This tree commemorates F/Sgt L Lissette
RNZAF pilot and the members of the crew of
Lancaster EM-F 207 Sqn, Spilsby, lost
Mailley le Camp 3/4 May 1944*

*This tree commemorates the crew of 57 Sqn,
lost 2-12-1943
F/O J A Williams, Pilot; P/O B P Dural, Nav;
Sgt J Chambers (Harvey) W/Op; Sgt E
Hibbert, Flt Eng; Sgt B Thomasberg, BA; Sgt E
W Graves, A/G; P/O A T Hook, A/G*

Towards the watch tower is a further **tree**,
donated by the Fenland branch of the Bomber
Command Association, and **memorial plaque**,
dedicated to the memory of all those who gave
their lives whilst serving with Bomber Command.

In the **cafe/shop** area are two **presentation
cups**, both bearing the name of the Gregory
Croft School, one the 57 Squadron Trophy, the

other the 630 Squadron Trophy. A number of
small aircraft components are mounted on a
board, on the front of which is a **plaque** dedicating the board to the memory of the Halifax and
their crews. A **silver metal bat** (possibly relating
to 9 Squadron), mounted on a base. A **portrait**
of Roy Chadwick, designer of the Lancaster,
with a plaque recording that it was unveiled on
30th April 1991 by Group Captain L Cheshire. A
**print** of a Lancaster is displayed, with underneath the inscription:

*To the memory of the air and groundcrews of
463 & 467 Squadrons
Royal Australian Air Force
'Forever in our thoughts'*

In the **RAF Escaping Society exhibition building** is the public house sign 'The Escape', which
formerly hung outside premises near Euston
railway station.

**Memorials to the units that operated from Elsham Wolds, inside the Anglian Water premises** (above) **and outside** (below).

## ELSHAM WOLDS (RAF)    112/TA041132

Signposted off the B1206 at the crossroads near an aerial mast, at the **Anglian Water Authority** treatment works, built on the edge of the former airfield site, at the end of one of the runways. In the entrance foyer of the main building is a **memorial plaque**, dedicated on 20th June 1975, with the badges of 1 Group and 103 Squadron and the inscription:

*RAF Elsham Wolds*
*Opened in Summer 1941 as a Bomber*
*Station in No 1 Group*
*It was the home of No 103 Squadron and*
*from Elsham Wolds until 1945 Wellington,*
*Halifax and Lancaster aircraft of No 103 and*
*other squadrons flew on bombing missions*
*against targets in Germany and Occupied*
*Europe*

A **panel**, from 'C' Flight of 33 Squadron, which operated from what was then RFC/RAF Elsham in the Great War. With the letters 'RAF' surmounted by a crown it reads:

*Elsham*
*'C' Flight 33rd Squadn*
*Per ardua ad astra*

Other items on display in the foyer are **boards** listing honours and awards of 103 Squadron, honours of 576 Squadron, and 103 Squadron, stations, commanding officers and aircraft types. There are photographs taken in May 1945 of 103 Squadron and 13 Base Major Servicing Section, and **plates** with the badges of 103 and 576 Squadrons.

    **Outside** the main building is a **memorial garden**, featuring the centre hub and two blades of a propeller unit. The numbers '103' and '576' are picked out in white stones, and the letters 'EW' and the shape of a pilot's flying badge formed by flower beds.

    A **memorial stone**, dedicated on 27th August 1989 replacing a plaque dedicated in 1981, standing at the front of the garden, with the badges of 103 and 576 Squadrons and the inscription:

*Royal Air Force Elsham Wolds*
*1941-1945*
*For those who made the great sacrifice*

## EPWORTH    112/SE780040

There has been a report of a **propeller blade** standing close by the A161 in the Epworth area.

## FALDINGWORTH    121/TF066848

In the **village church** (All Saints) on the A46 a **memorial plaque**, dedicated on 29th April 1995, is mounted on the wall of the north aisle, depicting the Polish Air Force ensign, with the inscription:

*Polskie Sily Powietrzne*
*In remembrance of the many men and*
*women of the Polish Air Force who served at*
*Faldingworth aerodrome from*
*1944 to 1947*
*Their sacrifice and endeavour in the cause of*
*freedom forms a bond between our two*
*countries that will always be recalled with*
*honour and with pride*
*Polska - Wielka Brytania*
*Za Nasza I Wasza Wolnosc*

## FALDINGWORTH (RAF/PAF)    121/TF028848

At the **Royal Ordnance Factory**, on an unclassified road between the A15 and the A46. In the conference room, together with a certificate giving details of the history of the station and airfield site is a framed **certificate**, with the badges of 300 and 305 Squadrons. Note that the certificates can only be viewed by prior arrangement, and permission is not automatic. The inscription reads:

*300 Dywizjon Bombowy*
*'Ziemi Mazowieckiej'*
*305 Dywizjon Bombowy*
*'Ziemi Wielkopolskiej'*
*Polskie Sily Powietrzne*

*RAF Faldingworth*
*300 Squadron of the Polish Air Force*
*operated from RAF Faldingworth*
*with Avro Lancasters between 1944-1946,*
*as part of No 1 Group Bomber Command.*
*In 1946 it was joined by 305 Squadron with de*
*Havilland Mosquitos, and both Squadrons*
*disbanded in January 1947.*

## FISKERTON       121/TF048720

At the **village church** (St Clement), on an unclassified road south of the A158. In the Lady Chapel in the south aisle is a **memorial plaque**, dedicated on 23rd August 1987, with the badges of 49 and 576 Squadrons and the inscription:

*In memory*
*of all who served at*
*RAF Fiskerton 1943-1945*
*Per ardua ad astra*

The **roll of honour** of 49 Squadron, dedicated on 24th April 1994, serves to the memory of those who died while serving with the unit at Scampton, Fiskerton and Fulbeck, 1939-45. A copy of the 49 Squadron roll of honour is available for viewing by visitors. Below the badge of 49 Squadron is the inscription:

*They died – that freedom might live*

The **badge** of 49 Squadron is displayed. This was presented to the Royal Observer Corps (ROC) by the 49 Squadron Association on 23rd August 1987. The **badge** of 576 Squadron, also presented to the ROC by members of 576 Squadron in August 1987. See also page 70.

## FULBECK       121/SK948504

At the **village church** (St Nicholas) on the A607. A **rose bush**, and a **plaque** presented by the 931st Air Refueling Group, USAF. The bush and plaque are close by the lychgate and village **war memorial**, and the churchyard contains an air force grave.

**Memorial to Flight Sergeant Ken White and those who flew from Fulbeck, never to return.**

In **Fulbeck Hall** (121/SK947505), signposted just off the A607, is a **memorial plaque** to personnel of the 1st Airborne Division who fought at the Battle of Arnhem, unveiled on 17th September 1994.

Fulbeck Hall was the headquarters of the 1st Airborne Division from October 1943 to September 1945. The former map room is known as the **Arnhem Room**. A special 50th anniversary exhibition took place in 1994 recreating the room as it was in the period prior to the Arnhem operation, and this will be a permanent exhibition from 1995. The Hall is open to the public during the summer months (times vary). Admission charge. Telephone 01400 272205

## FULBECK (RAF/USAAF)       121/SK909510

On an unclassified road south of the A17, at the entrance road to the **former airfield**, set on a base in the shape of a propeller is a **memorial stone**. An inscription at the foot of the memorial stone records that it is the Flight Sergeant Ken White Memorial, erected by the Bomber Airfield Society in 1988. It carries the badges of Bomber Command and the Bomber Airfield Society and the inscription:

*In memory of all who flew from*
*RAF Fulbeck*
*never to return*
*1940-45*

It is proposed that a **plaque** to the crew of Avro Lancaster III ME408 of 49 Squadron, lost on 4th April 1945, will be placed on the memorial.

## GOXHILL (RAF/USAAF)       113/TA111222

On the north western edge of the **former airfield** site, on an unclassified road north east of Goxhill village and of the B1206. A **propeller blade** mounted on a stone cairn, and a **memorial plaque** with the badges of the United States of America and the United States 8th Air Force. Between the badge, a Lockheed P-38 Lightning is depicted, and two hands clasped in greeting are engraved above the bottom line on the plaque. The inscription reads:

*United States Army Air Force*
*No 345 Base Goxhill*
*Fighter Training Group*
*June 1942 — February 1945*
*'Gone but not forgotten'*

In addition, **two further plaques** are fixed to each side of the cairn. That on the right records that the memorial was unveiled on 9th September 1984 and:

*This tribute was organised and constructed by*
*the residents of Goxhill with the help of their*
*friends on behalf of the USAAF*
*servicemen who served on this airbase*

That on the left notes that the propeller blade is from P-38 Lightning 42-67199 from the base, and that the aircraft had crashed nearby on 26th May 1944. The pilot, 2nd Lieutenant L A Ferrara, was killed. It also records that:

*It represents the high price our countries paid for freedom*

The plaques on the memorial are not the originals; the centre and left plaques being replacements and the right almost certainly a replacement as well. The Lightning was from the 554th Fighter Training Squadron, of the 496th Fighter Training Group. The original plaque on the left recorded that the propeller blade had been recovered by the Humberside Aircraft Preservation Society in September 1983. This plaque was removed from the memorial during 1991, following what was reported to be an unfortunate local difference of opinion and became the subject of 'editing', the society name being machined off and the plaque replaced.

**The Goxhill memorial, P-38 Lightning propeller blade atop an impressive cairn.**

## GRANTHAM  130/SK916356

**Grantham Museum**, on St Peter's Hill in the town centre, holds a number of aviation items, some of which were previously exhibited at the 5 Group Heritage Air Museum, which was operated by the Grantham Aviation Society. Opening hours are May to September 10am to 5pm Monday to Saturday and October to April 10am to 5pm Tuesday to Saturday (closed 12.30pm to 1.30pm). The museum is open on bank holiday Mondays, but closed for the Christmas/New Year bank holiday days and is normally closed on Good Friday. Admission charge. Telephone 01476 68783.

Inside is a **memorial plaque**, having a winged 'star and bar' badge with three Douglas C-47 Skytrains depicted. The plaque is one of two presented by the 61st Troop Carrier Group (TCG) to the people of Grantham before it left USAAF Barkston Heath in March 1945 (see also the Nettleham entry), and was previously held in the Guildhall. Note that the plaque, in the care of South Kesteven District Council, was placed on display in the museum during 1993. This arrangement might not be permanent, and it may be relocated in the adjoining council buildings. It is possible that viewing may then be by prior arrangement only.

The inscription on the memorial plaque reads:

*Sixty First Troop Carrier Group*
*United States Army Air Forces*
*Barkston Heath,*
*Lincolnshire*
*1944-1945*

*In appreciation of the fellowship, hospitality, and understanding shown by the people and officials of the town of Grantham to all of us, who far from our own homes, spent so many days in yours while we were joined in destroying the tyrannical power which threatened both*

*This testimonial is presented by the officers and men of the Sixty First Troop Carrier Group*

In **St Vincent's** (130/SK925351), on St Vincent's Road, south east of the town centre is a **plaque**, with the badge of 5 Group, commemorating the Group's tenure in the building. St Vincent's was the headquarters of 5 Group and is now the offices of Suter plc. The plaque can only be viewed by prior arrangement, and permission is not automatic.

In the town **cemetery** (130/SK921355), on Harrowby Road east of the town centre is a Commonwealth War Graves Commission **cross of sacrifice** and it also contains a number of air force graves and a memorial to civilian casualties of the Second World War.

In the **headquarters** of 47F (Grantham) Squadron Air Training Corps, Trigg's Yard (130/SK913360) off Watergate, in the town centre, is a **commemorative plaque**. (Note that the plaque can only be viewed by prior arrangement, and permission is not automatic.) The inscription reads:

*This building was opened by*
*Air Vice Marshal F D Hughes*
*cb cbe dso dfc afc ma dl*
*on 30th July 1989*
*in the 50th anniversary year of*
*47F Sqn Air Training Corps, Grantham*

## GREAT STEEPING  122/TF441643

In the **village church** (All Saints) off the B1195 is a circular **memorial plaque**, mounted on the south wall of the nave, dedicated on 21st May 1989, with the badge of 44 Squadron and the inscription:

*44 (Rhodesia) Squadron*
*Royal Air Force*
*In memory of those who served*
*Royal Air Force Spilsby*
*Sept 1944 – July 1945*
*'We will remember them'*

A large **memorial plaque**, dedicated on 8th May 1992, is mounted on the north wall of the nave. It carries the badge of 207 Squadron and the inscription:

*Between October 1943 and October 1945
No 207 Squadron Royal Air Force was based
here at Spilsby aerodrome, whose boundaries
encompassed this Church of All Saints at
Great Steeping
Until 27th April 1945, flying from here the
Squadron's Lancaster bombers, each with
seven crewmen, took the battle to the enemy,
mostly by night.
Until 6th June 1944 this was the only way in
which Great Britain could strike out from
these shores in its own defence and in the
cause of freedom. In this period, 511 men of
No 207 Squadron were killed, 104 of whom
have no known grave.
They included men from Great Britain,
Canada, Australia, New Zealand, the USA, the
Netherlands, and Eire, and 12 members of the
ground staff.
133 more did not return from operations, of
whom 109 became prisoners of war until May
1945, and 24 evaded capture.*

*'Lest we forget'*

At the west end of the nave is the **roll of honour** of 207 Squadron, held in a display cabinet. This was dedicated on 8th May 1992, and deposited by the 207 Squadron Association. (See also 'Late Additions' on page 70.) Within the cover is the inscription:

**The roll of honour of 207 Squadron, kept in the village church at Great Steeping. It is typical of many to be found in the county. Often a copy is available for reference.**

*Herein are the names
of 511 of the Squadron's men who were
killed in action
In addition are those of 133 of the
Squadron's men, whose aircraft having been
shot down, were taken prisoners of war
and 109 of the Squadron's men,
whose aircraft having been shot down,
were able to evade capture, and return to the
United Kingdom*

## GRIMSBY                                    113/TA273084

In a **local church** (St Augustine of Hippo), on Legsby Avenue south of the town centre, is a **wooden panel** in memory of Lieutenant W B Wood of the Royal Flying Corps, and of his brother. The panel also acts as a memorial to fellow old boys of St James' School.

In the **parish church** (SS Mary and James — 113/TA266092), in St James' Square in the town centre, the **war memorial** includes separate panels for personnel of the Royal Flying Corps, Royal Naval Air Service, and Royal Air Force. Four windows in the north transept were designed by Hugh Easton, who also designed the window of the Royal Air Force Chapel in Westminster Abbey.

In the **cemetery**, off Scartho Road, the A16, south of the town centre (113/TA270072) is a Commonwealth War Graves Commission **cross of sacrifice**. A Commonwealth War Graves Commission **stone of remembrance** — the only one in Lincolnshire — is also in the cemetery, together with a number of air force graves.

In the **town hall** (113/TA271092), in Town Hall Square, in the town centre is a **stained glass window**, the Victory Window, and a memorial plaque with the inscription:

*To honour and record the service
of men and women
of Grimsby 1939-1945*

The window, unveiled on 21st December 1949, is of three lights and is above the main staircase. The centre panel displays the badges of the

**Stained glass window in Grimsby town hall.**

Royal Air Force, Fleet Air Arm pilot's badge, Auxiliary Territorial Service, RAF cap badge, Women's Royal Naval Service, Royal Navy, Merchant Navy, the Lincolnshire Regiment, the British Army, and the emblems of England, Scotland, Ireland, and Wales. The left panel displays the badges of the Royal Observer Corps, National Fire Service, Women's Land Army, St John Ambulance, and Borough of Grimsby Special Constabulary. The panel on the right displays the badges of the Minesweeping/Anti-Submarine Service, Civil Defence, Women's Voluntary Service, British Red Cross Society, and Grimsby Borough Police.

Displayed by the window are a number of **ensigns**, including those of the RAF and Royal and Merchant Navies. Two further windows, unveiled on 14th July 1992, show the life of Grimsby. One includes an English Electric Lightning and a BAe 146 airliner.

A **panel** in one of the windows of the Council Chamber depicts the badge of 12 Squadron. An engraved **panel** records the granting of the Honorary Freedom of Grimsby, and includes 12 Squadron (in 1954) and RAF Binbrook (in 1966), together with the unit badges.

A small **plaque**, with the painted depiction of a pilot's flying badge of the Royal Air Force, presented by RAF Elsham Wolds in 1941. The plaque, on the wall near the reception area, is one of a number of **badges** which also include those of 12 Squadron, 460 Squadron, and the United States Army Air Force.

A **silver model of a lion**, presented to the County Borough of Grimsby by RAF Binbrook, 1st April 1966. The piece was presented to mark the granting of the Freedom of Grimsby to the Station, a lion being depicted in the badge of RAF Binbrook.

In the Mayor's Parlour is a **model** of an English Electric Lightning, and a **plaque** on the base recording that it was presented to the Mayor and the council to commemorate the lasting friendship between RAF Binbrook and Great Grimsby. In the civic insignia is the **Binbrook Sword**, presented by RAF Binbrook on 4th October 1988. Note that not all of the above items are on public display and prior application may be necessary to view them.

In the **Welholme Galleries** (113/TA276086), on Hainton Avenue (B1213), south of the town centre is a **model** of one of the Grimsby presentation Spitfires, believed to be R7231 'Grimsby II'. The model is part of the Grimsby museum collection currently held in store, and viewing is not possible.

### GRIMSBY (RAF)      113/TA283030

In a lay-by on the western side of the A16, at the northern end of the Holton-le-Clay bypass, on

**Remembering RAF Grimsby** (above) **the 100 Squadron memorial and** (below) **'The Jug & Bottle'.**

the former airfield site, is a **memorial stone**, dedicated on 7th November 1978 and erected by members of Bravo 3 Post Fulstow, Royal Observer Corps. It has the badge and motto of 100 Squadron and the inscription:

> *Do not attack the hornets nest*
> *No 100 Squadron Royal Air Force*
> *Waltham, Grimsby*
> *December 1942 – April 1945*
> *Honour the brave*

**'The Jug & Bottle'** (113/TA284020) a public house, just off the A16 at the southern end of the Holton-le-Clay bypass. Inside is a framed **certificate**, with the inscription:

> *This pub was named after*
> *a World War Two Lancaster bomber*
> *called 'Jug and Bottle'*
> *which in 1944 stood on the site of this*
> *building as part of the 100 Squadron*
> *operating from RAF Waltham.*

The certificate also gives details of the official opening of the pub, which took place on 14th April 1992. The aircraft was PA177, 'HW-J²' 'Jig Two' of 100 Squadron. Throughout the pub are many photographs, including the opening ceremony and the unveiling of the 100 Squadron memorial, and also the badge of 100 Squadron. Outside the **pub sign** depicts Lancaster I PA177, the original 'Jug & Bottle'.

### HALTON HOLEGATE      122/TF416652

At **'The Bell'** public house, on the B1195, the **pub sign** displays the pub itself with a Lancaster flying overhead with the names of 44 and 207 Squadrons underneath.

### HARLAXTON      130/SK895323

At **Harlaxton Manor**, off the A607, set in the grounds of the gardens is the Pegasus **badge** of the 1st Airborne Division. The gardens are normally open to the public in the summer.

## HARPSWELL      112/SK936899

In the **village church** (St Chad), off the A631 near its junction with the B1398 a **roll of honour** in memory of personnel from RAF Hemswell is mounted on the wall of the south aisle. Standing beneath the roll of honour is a **flower stand**, and a plaque with the inscription 'RAF Hemswell Reunions'. The churchyard contains a number of air force graves.

## HARRINGTON      122/TF406733

A memorial to the crew of 12 Squadron Lancaster PB476 was dedicated on 5th March 1995 – see 'Late Additions' on page 70.

## HECKINGTON      130/TF143441

The **village church** (St Andrew), is on an unclassified road off the B1394. In the south aisle is a **memorial plaque** to personnel of the 1st Airlanding Anti-Tank Battery, Royal Artillery, particularly those lost in the Arnhem operation.

Also in the south aisle is a **stained glass window** erected in memory of villagers lost in the Great War, together with a plaque commemorating those lost in the Second World War. Outside, the cemetery contains a number of air force graves.

## HEMSWELL (RAF)      112/SK947897

The former airfield is now part of the new village of Hemswell Cliff. The technical site has also been developed for a variety of commercial and retail uses.

By the **former main gate**, on the A631 west of Caenby Corner is a **memorial stone**, with the badge of 170 Squadron, depicting an Avro Lancaster beneath the translation of the squadron motto 'To see but not be seen'. An inscription on the base records that the stone is in memory of all those who did not return, 1944-45. The memorial was erected by the 170 Squadron Reunion Association and was dedicated in ceremony held in June 1985.

A joint **memorial** has been proposed, to all who served at RAF Hemswell – see 'Late Additions' on page 70.

The **Bomber County Aviation Museum** (112/SK948901) is located to the rear the former station headquarters building, and is open all year. Opening hours are 10am to 5pm Sundays, special open days, and also at other times by arrangement. The museum is operated by the Hemswell Aviation Society and has a range of display items (including Bristol Sycamore, de Havilland Vampire, English Electric Canberra, Hawker Hunter). The museum, established by the Humberside Aircraft Preservation Society and known previously as the Humberside Aviation Museum, was earlier at Cleethorpes and Elsham Hall. The museum includes a shop, access and facilities for disabled people, toilets, car parking. Admission free. Telephone 01427 668809.

**Memorial to 170 Squadron at the former RAF Hemswell site.**

A new public house in the former airmen's mess block (112/SK950902) is named **'The Lincoln Inn'**. The sign displays a silver-painted Avro Lincoln. The former station headquarters building is named Gibson House. Nearby are the Lancaster Nursing Home and Blenheim House.

## HIBALDSTOW (RAF)      112/SE985010

It is understood that there has been a proposal for a **memorial** on the former airfield site, on the A15.

## HOLBEACH      131/TF358248

At the **village church** (All Saints), on the A151, is a **tree** in memory of Sergeant R E Herd. In the **town cemetery** is an air force grave.

## IMMINGHAM      113/TA183140

The **town museum**, in the Resources Centre on Margaret Street in the town centre is normally open all year. Opening hours are 10am to 4pm Monday to Friday. Admission charge. Telephone 01469 577066.

The museum holds the United States 'Stars and Stripes' **flag** which flew over the 1914-18 Naval Air Station at nearby Killingholme. Also exhibited are a number of contemporary photographs and a section of hull from what is believed to be a Felixstowe flying-boat which had been on the station.

## KEDDINGTON      122/TF345887

In the **village church** (St Margaret), on an unclassified road north east of Louth is a **plaque** on the organ recording that it is in memory of Flight Lieutenant C S Staniland, former test pilot for Fairey Aircraft. He is buried in the churchyard.

Located on the site of RAF Kelstern, the memorial to 625 Squadron includes the Lancaster squadron's motto : 'We Avenge'.

## KELSTERN (RAF)　　　113/TF254920

At 'Kelstern crossroads', north of the village on an unclassified road between the A631 and B1203 stands a **memorial stone**. Located on the former airfield site and dedicated on 25th October 1964, this was the first memorial of its type in the county. Erected by the 625 Squadron Association, it is in the care of 1228 (Louth) Squadron Air Training Corps. See also 'Late Additions' on page 70. The memorial carries the badge of 625 Squadron and the inscription:

> *625 Squadron Royal Air Force*
> *October 1943 – April 1945*
> *'We avenge'*

## KIRMINGTON　　　113/TA106113

In the **village church** (St Helen), on an unclassified road off the A18, is a **memorial plaque**. Originally dedicated on 7th April 1956, the plaque is in the sanctuary, carrying the badge of 166 Squadron and inscription:

> *In proud and undying memory of*
> *members of 166 Squadron RAF*
> *who flew from Kirmington airfield*
> *and did not return from*
> *their last sortie 1943-1945*
> *This tablet was placed here*
> *by their comrades*

The **roll of honour** of 166 Squadron, is held in a display cabinet beneath the memorial plaque. Within the cover is a dedication:

> *I dedicate this book*
> *to the men of 166 Squadron RAF Kirmington*
> *who 'failed to return', many of whom*
> *have no known graves especially the crew of*
> *Lancaster LM390 lost on a raid to Magdebourg*
> *January 21st/22nd 1944*
> *one of this crew,*
> *Sgt L Collins, being my uncle*
> *[signed] David Cressey.*

> *They ascended to realms of*
> *highest endeavour, never*
> *to return, yet to remain*
> *with us for ever*
> *in our hearts.*

On an unclassified road in Kirmington **village** (113/TA105114), opposite the church, is a **garden,** and a **memorial plaque** mounted on a stone pillar with the badge of 166 Squadron. The Memorial was dedicated on 3rd September 1988 and carries the inscription:

> *'Ye that live mid England's pastures green*
> *think on us and what might have been'*

> *This memorial is dedicated to all the men*
> *and women who served with*
> *166 Squadron at Royal Air Force Kirmington*

*1943-1945, of whom 921 gave their lives*
*that we may be free.*
*We do not forget the villagers who took us*
*into their hearts and homes. We will be*
*forever grateful for their comradeship and*
*humanity, for with their caring help we stood*
*together to conquer tyranny*

*'We will remember them'*

Opposite the church in Kirmington village is a memorial to the dead of 166 Squadron and to the people of the area.

Close by the 166 Squadron memorial is **'The Marrowbone and Cleaver'** public house (113/TA104114), the **sign** depicting Lancaster 'AS-A' of 166 Squadron (to whom the pub was known as 'The Chopper').

Inside the terminal building at Humberside International Airport is the Robert Blackburn mural (left) and the original station bell from RAF Kirmington (above).

## KIRMINGTON (RAF)  112/TA094109

The former RAF Kirmington is now Humberside International Airport — signposted on the A18. The restoration of the 'south bank' to Lincolnshire in 1996 might lead to a proposal for a name change. In the passenger hall of the **terminal building**, is a **memorial plaque**, with the badge of 166 Squadron and the inscription:

*166 Squadron Royal Air Force*
*This plaque was presented by Humberside*
*County Council to commemorate the heavy*
*losses sustained by 166 Squadron which oper-*
*ated from this airfield between January 1943*
*and May 1945*

A framed copy of the **badge** of 166 Squadron, with above an RAF cap badge, and below a plaque is displayed, presented to the airport by the 166 Squadron Association in 1990. The **station bell**, RAF Kirmington, together with a commemorative plaque with the inscription:

*This is the Original Station Bell from*
*Royal Air Force Kirmington.*

*166 Squadron RAF operated from this base*
*between 19th February 1942 and*
*28th November 1945.*

A framed illuminated **certificate**, which has both English and Dutch text, carries the flags of Canada, Australia, New Zealand, the UK, the USA, Poland, and Holland, together with the badges of the towns. A Lancaster dropping supplies is in the background. The certificate was donated on behalf of the 166 Squadron and Manna Associations, and below it is recorded that aircraft of 166 Squadron took part in Operation MANNA, dropping supplies to the Dutch people between 29th April and 8th May 1945. Note that the certificate is only normally displayed (together with a photograph of 166 Squadron) for reunions. It can only be viewed by prior arrangement, and permission is not automatic. The certificate carries the inscription:

*29th April – 8th May 1945 Charter*
*In thankful remembrance to Your action of*
*Courage and Humanity fulfilled by you and your*
*friends in the last days of the War in 1945*
*flying food provided to starving*
*Holland*

*'The darkest hour is before the dawn'*

*In the sure convection* [sic] *of remaining*
*friendship presentated* [sic] *to you*
*by the population of Rijnsburg, Katwijk,*
*Valkenburg-ZH and by the home-club*
*In het Gareel*
*1st May 1985*

In addition there are a number of commemorative plaques marking the development of the civil airport and the opening of facilities. Also in the passenger hall is a large display **mural** commemorating Robert Blackburn whose factory at Brough was across the River Humber near Hull. The mural depicts a facial of Blackburn, his 1909 monoplane and a Buccaneer. Beneath the mural is a panel giving details.

## KIRTON IN LINDSEY  112/SK934985

The **village church** (St Andrew), is off the B1398. The burial ground contains a number of air force graves. A **memorial plaque** in the bell tower lists those founder contributors to the bells, and has this inscription:

*The Royal Air Force
and Royal Artillery bells
Dedicated 1982*

*That in everything God may be glorified*

*1 Peter 4 v.11*

## KIRTON IN LINDSEY (RAF)  112/SK942979

Signposted on the B1400, the **headquarters building**, Rapier Barracks, holds a **certificate**. Note the certificate can only be viewed by prior arrangement, and permission is not automatic. The certificate, with the badges of 302, 303, 306, 307, 316, and 317 Squadrons, is inscribed:

*302 Dywizjon Mysliwski
'Poznanski'
303 Dywizjon Mysliwski
'Warszawski im Tadeusza Kosciuszki'
306 Dywizjon Mysliwski
'Torunski'
307 Nocny Dywizjon Mysliwski
'Lwowski'
316 Dywizjon Mysliwski
'Warszawski'
317 Dywizjon Mysliwski
'Wilenski'
Polskie Sily Powietrzne
Krolewskie Sily Powietrzne*

*302, 303, 306, 307, 316, and 317 Squadrons
of the Polish Air Force operated from RAF Kirton
in Lindsey between
1940-1943. With the exception of 307 Squadron,
the units all flew Spitfire fighters.
307 Squadron was a night fighter unit, and
was the only Polish Air Force Squadron
to be formed in Lincolnshire,
at Kirton in Lindsey in September 1940.
Amongst its original aircraft was the Defiant
aircraft N1671 now on display in the
Royal Air Force Museum at Hendon.*

*Za nasza wolnosc i wasza*

*For our freedom and yours*

**Boulton Paul Defiant I N1671 on show at the RAF Museum, Hendon. It served with 307 Squadron from Kirton in Lindsey from September to November 1940, a fact noted on a memorial certificate held at what is now Rapier Barracks.** Alan Curry

## LAUGHTERTON  121/SK838761

On the **village green**, on the A1133, is the **Trentside Memorial**. The memorial was dedicated on 16th July 1994. The Stirling plaque is to a 1661 Heavy Conversion Unit crew. A propeller blade and reduction gear mounted on a stone cairn, and plaques on two faces with the inscriptions:

*In memory of F/O G C Brown RCAF,
Sgt J Corless RAF Crew of Lancaster LM292
from 103 Squadron RAF Elsham Wold
killed in action near Fenton 8th August 1944*

*On sun tipped wing they loved to fly,
Into the wide unmeasured sky*

*In memory of F/O F S Bradbury RAF (VR), F/O G
W Rankin RAF (VR), F/O W R Clayton RAF (VR)
Sgt W H Miller RAF (VR),
Sgt J A Micallef RAF (VR)*

*Crew of Short Stirling EH940 based at RAF
Winthorpe killed in action at Kettlethorpe 21st
June 1944*

## LEADENHAM (RFC)  121/SK964519

On an unclassified road, north of the A17 is a **marker panel**, with an RFC roundel, noting the site of the former RFC Leadenham. The panel is one of those placed by North Kesteven District Council for its Airfield Trail. The former airfield nearby was a home defence station in the Great War.

## LINCOLN

The housing estates of **Birchwood** and **Doddington Park** are built on the site of the former RAF Skellingthorpe, and the various memorials there are listed under the station name.

On Castle Hill, close to the main gateway of **Lincoln Castle** (121/SK975718) is the **Airborne Memorial Garden**, dedicated in 1989 to all Allied parachute forces killed in action. At the entrance to the garden is a **commemorative name plaque**. In the garden is a **memorial stone** to personnel of the British and Allied Airborne Forces, dedicated in 1992.

Also in the garden is a **plaque** from the French parachute association. The door to the garden is normally locked, but the key can be obtained from the gatehouse of the castle.

As might be expected, **Lincoln Cathedral** (121/SK978718 — the Cathedral Church of the Blessed Virgin Mary of Lincoln), north of the city centre, contains many memorials to the aerial activity of the county. One of three service chapels (Royal Navy — St Andrew, Army — St George) in the north transept, the **Airmen's Chapel** (St Michael) was rededicated in 1923. Holy Communion is celebrated in the chapel each Thursday morning. In the chapel are three **RAF memorial books**. Normally, one of the books is held in a glass fronted display cabinet in the chapel. The 1 Group and 5 Group books were dedicated on 8th November 1949, and contain the names of 21,000 personnel. The third book covers personnel from 6, 7, 91, 92 and 93 Groups. Each book commences with an illuminated page noting that it is in memory of those aircrew who served in that group and never returned from operations. The three books are held in a **wooden casket**, in front of which is a stone set into the floor. The casket carries a plaque with the inscription:

*These memorial books*
*contain the names of 25,611 men,*
*who flew from Royal Air Force stations*
*in or near Lincolnshire*
*during the Second World War,*
*and never returned.*

*They include 200 from New Zealand,*
*1,140 from Australia, 1,233 from Canada,*
*approximately 90 from Southern Rhodesia,*
*and 687 members of the Polish Air Force.*

*All were members of*
*No 1, 5, 6, 7, 91, 92, 93 (OTU) Group,*
*Bomber Command.*

The east window (north), was dedicated on 8th May 1954 as the **Bomber Command Memorial**. A stained glass window incorporating the badge of Bomber Command, St Michael slaying

**The altar of the Airmen's Chapel in Lincoln Cathedral.**

the dragon of evil, two figures (representing air and ground crews) and Lancasters in plan form. The east window (south), dedicated in 1953, is the **New Zealand Memorial**. A stained glass window incorporating an aircrew figure, the cathedral, and the arms of the City of Lincoln. The **Flying Training Command** stained glass window, the north east window, was dedicated in 1958. It incorporates the badge of Flying Training Command and depicts the figures of a pilot and a cadet from the RAF College. Adjacent is a commemorative plaque, noting that the window was unveiled by HM Queen Elizabeth II, accompanied by the Duke of Edinburgh, on 27th June 1958. The **north west window**, dedicated in 1966, is in memory of a Rhodesian airman and incorporates the badge of the Royal Rhodesian Air Force.

There are **two benches**, one with the arms of Australia and the words 'In Loving Memory of

Our Noble Boys' the other, with the arms of Southern Rhodesia and the words 'In Proud and Loving Memory of Our Boys from Southern Rhodesia'.

The **Queen's Colour** for the Central Flying School, laid up in 1992. Also within are the **standards** for 8, 27, 83 and 617 Squadrons, an RAF ensign and a Royal Australian Air Force ensign. The standard of 83 Squadron has a **memorial plaque** with the inscription:

*The standard of*
*83 Squadron Pathfinder Force RAF*
*hangs here in memory*
*of those who flew from Lincolnshire*
*in the Second World War*
*and failed to return*

On the altar are a **silver cross and candlesticks**, commemorating Squadron Leader H E Maudslay and his crew, killed in the attack on the Ruhr dams in 1943. There is a **memorial plaque** to Air Vice Marshal Sir Edward Rice, former Air Officer Commanding 1 Group, Bomber Command. The credence table bears a small **plaque** in memory of Sergeant H Dracass. The **hanging candelabra**, a gift from the Air Training Corps in Lincolnshire, was dedicated in 1949.

The **standard** of the Royal Air Force Escaping Society is to be laid up in the chapel in September 1995. It is understood that consideration is being given to a proposal for a **memorial** to personnel of the Polish Air Force.

Also in the chapel are the badge of the RAF, the **badges** of Fighter Command, Bomber Command, Flying Training Command, Maintenance Command, 1 Group, 5 Group, the arms of the RAF College, and a Bishop's chair presented by the people of the City of Pietermaritzburg.

Lincoln's **Central Library** (121/SK977713 – on Free School Lane in the city centre) holds the **Lincoln Memory Book**, displayed in a glass case mounted on a stone base. Originally dedicated in 1922, listing citizens of Lincoln who had lost their lives (including those in the RFC and RAF) in the Great War was subsequently added to after the Second World War.

The library building is being rebuilt and will not reopen until 1996. The book is currently in store, and viewing is not possible. Copies of the entries are held on microfilm and may be inspected in the reference library which is temporarily housed in the Greyfriars building on Broadgate (121/SK978713).

**Christ's Hospital School** (121/SK987724) on Wragby Road (the A158) north east of the city centre holds the **Wickenby Trophy**, a scale model of Avro Lancaster I ME756 'PH-N' of 12 Squadron. It was given to the school by the Wickenby Register, the 12 and 626 Squadrons' Association, and is presented annually to a sixth form student for outstanding achievement in any field. Note that the trophy can only be viewed by prior arrangement, and permission is not automatic. A plaque on it has the inscription:

*Presented to*
*the Lincoln Christ's Hospital School by the*
*Wickenby Register*
*September 1983*
*to commemorate those who gave*
*their lives in the operation of*
*Lancasters from Wickenby Airfield*
*between 1943 and 1945*

**Memorial plaque inside the County Hospital, Lincoln.**

In the Lincolnshire County Council offices, **County Hall**, on Newland west of the city centre (121/SK972714) is the **roll of honour** of 50 and 61 Squadrons for 1939-45. Note that this can only be viewed by prior arrangement, and permission is not automatic. Outside the offices is a **rose garden**, which commemorates the 50th anniversary of the D-Day landings.

In the **County Hospital**, (signposted) on Greetwell Road north east of the city centre (121/SK991718). Adjacent to the chapel is a **memorial plaque**, with the inscription:

*In memory of*
*officers, NCOs, and other ranks*
*of 5 (Bomber) Group RAF*
*who lost their lives*
*Sept 1939 – May 1945*

Originally mounted above a bed endowed to the hospital, the plaque is amongst several displayed near the main entrance. Another **plaque** notes that the bed was endowed by the US Services Fund for the use of officers and men of the navy, army and air force who served in the Great War. Other plaques include the 'Tank' bed, recording the design and construction of the world's first tanks in Lincoln by William Foster & Co in 1916. The hospital also holds the Lincolnshire Yeomanry memorial. In the maternity wing mounted on the wall outside Nocton Ward is the **badge** of RAF Hospital Nocton Hall.

In the **Eastgate Hotel**, now named the Lincoln Posthouse Hotel, on Eastgate (121/SK979719) immediately to the north of the Cathedral, mounted by the reception is the **badge** of the Manna Association of Bomber Command. The badge depicts the silhouette of an Avro Lancaster dropping supplies, on the background of the flag of the Netherlands. On the scroll beneath is the motto *Voedsel uit de Hemel*, which translates as 'Food from the Sky'. The badge is inscribed:

*Presented to*
*the Lincoln Forte Crest Hotel in recognition*
*of the hospitality afforded*
*The Manna Association at their*
*Annual Reunion 25th April 1992*

In the foyer the **Grand Hotel**, on St Mary's Street in the city centre (121/SK977709) is a **painting** of two Lancasters of 153 Squadron, with the **badge** of 153 Squadron, carrying the date 4th April 1945. There are two inscriptions:

*Lancaster  Mk I P4-U RA544*
*Wg Cdr F S Powley dfc afc Pilot*
*Sgt C F Sadler F/Eng*
*FS L G Sims Nav*
*FS W Higgins A/B*
*WO A S Dickson W/Op*
*FS C Madden MU/G*
*Sgt I A Birrell R/G*

*Lancaster Mk I P4-R NX563*
*Flt Lt A J Winder Pilot*
*Sgt G E Thomson F/Eng*
*Fg Off L C Turner Nav*
*Fg Off E O Griffith A/B*
*FS J B Coffey W/Op*
*Fg Off A S Blake MU/G*
*FS R Neal R/G*

Both aircraft in the painting were lost in a mining operation on 4th/5th April 1945. No.153 Squadron reunions have been held at the hotel since 1955, and a plaque on the frame records that the painting was presented on 8th May 1993 by 'The Doomies'. Also on display are photographs of 'A' Flight and 'B' Flight of 153 Squadron at Scampton in June 1945, and a colour photograph of the BBMF Lancaster overflying Lincoln (and the Grand Hotel).

In the **Guildhall** (121/SK976713) , on Saltergate in the city centre, the city insignia collection is held, including many air force memorial items. Note that the Guildhall is open to the public on the first Saturday of each month, when these items may be viewed. At all other times they can only be viewed by prior arrangement, and permission is not automatic. A **memorial plaque** to the crew of a Lancaster presented to the Deputy Mayor when attending a service at Hamont. The plaque also carries a small plate with the inscription:

*Limburgse Vrienden VD*
*Geallieerde Luchtmacht*

A **silver salver**, with the arms of the City of Lincoln and the badge of RAF Waddington, presented by the station upon its receipt of the honorary Freedom of the City, 25th April 1959. A **gilt model** of a Lancaster, presented by RAF Scampton on 14th May 1993 to commemorate its granting of the Freedom of the City. Also a copy of the **scroll** recording the granting of the Freedom of the City to RAF Scampton, dated 14th May 1993.

There are two **silver models**, both commissioned by Lincoln City Council to commemorate the service rendered to the RAF. The first is of a **Lancaster**, dated 20th January 1984, bearing the serial number PA474, the Lancaster of the Battle of Britain Memorial Flight adopted by the City, and coded 'AJ-G' (617 Squadron). The second is a **Vulcan**, dated 1st December 1983, which carries the serial number XM607, that of the Vulcan on display at RAF Waddington.

The Guildhall houses many other items presented to the city. They include many service **badges** on display, including RAF Waddington, RAF Scampton, the Central Flying School, Inspectorate of Recruiting, School of Recruit Training, RAF Police, RAF Aerobatic Team, 617 Squadron, 2503 (County of Lincoln) Squadron, 204 (City of Lincoln) Squadron Air Training Corps, other NATO units, and the Royal Air Forces Association. There are also a number of **paintings** depicting aircraft. The Guildhall also holds the ship's bell of HMS *Lincoln*, and the following specific commemorative items.

A **plaque** with the badges of 463 and 467 Squadrons, Royal Australian Air Force, dated May 1975. The **badge** of 411 Squadron, Royal Canadian Air Force, presented to the citizens of Lincoln on the occasion of the 50th anniversary of the unit, 16th June 1991.

The **badge** of the Oklahoma Air National Guard, with a picture of an LTV A-7 Corsair II, thanking the city for its wonderful hospitality. The **badges** of the 124th Tactical Fighter Squadron and the 132nd Tactical Fighter Wing, Iowa Air National Guard, thanking the city for outstanding hospitality, 8th May to 8th June 1985. The base on which the badges and plaque are mounted is in the shape of the state of Iowa's boundary.

A framed copy of the **badge** of 2729 (City of Lincoln) Squadron Royal Auxiliary Air Force, presented to the City of Lincoln, to mark the occasion of the Squadron receiving the City Crest on 26th November 1988. A **painting** of the British Airways Boeing 747-436 airliner 'City of Lincoln' G-BNLT, presented to the city by the crew, 16th May 1993.

On a shop-front, on the **High Street** (south of the Stonebow – 121/SK976712) in the city centre is a **memorial plaque**, with the arms of the City of Lincoln marking the site of a famous public house. The 'Saracen's Head' was perhaps better known in its day as the 'Snake Pit'. The plaque was unveiled on 21st May 1993, and is mounted high on the wall of a shop.

The plaque was the first of a series marking out famous people and places as part of a heritage trail for visitors to Lincoln. It reads:

**Plaque in Lincoln High Street marking the location of the 'Saracen's Head' – a famous RAF 'watering hole'.**

*City of Lincoln*
*The Saracen's Head*
*Near this site was the*
*Saracen's Head Hotel.*
*A favourite watering hole for thousands of*
*RAF and Allied airmen and women*
*who served on Lincolnshire airfields*
*in World War II.*
*The hotel regrettably closed in 1959.*

In **The Lawn Visitor Centre**, the former hospital on Union Road north of the city centre (121/SK973719) can be found the 1939-45 **roll of honour** of 50 and 61 Squadrons, dedicated on 2nd June 1991. This was previously in the Guildhall. It is held in a **memorial cabinet**, placed on display in June 1994. The cabinet is located in the hallway of the original main entrance, adjoining the Willis Suite, and also holds a copy of the roll of honour for viewing by visitors. It displays the **badges** of 50 Squadron and 61 Squadron, and a panel with the inscription:

*I Bear You on Eagles Wings,*
*and Brought You*
*unto Myself*
*Ex.19:4*

A small **museum**, centred around 50 Squadron and 61 Squadron at RAF Skellingthorpe, opened in May 1995. It will also include detail on other squadrons of 1 Group and 5 Group. It is understood that it will display items currently held in store at the Manser School, on the former RAF Skellingthorpe site. The roll of honour of 50 and 61 Squadrons and the memorial cabinet are to move into the museum.

In the **Museum of Lincolnshire Life**, on Burton Road north of the city centre (121/SK972722) are a small number of aviation items on display, primarily relating to the city's aircraft industry in the Great War. Opening hours are 10am to 5.30pm Monday to Saturday, all year; Sunday May to September 10am to 5.30pm and October to April 2pm to 5.30pm. The museum is closed for the Christmas/New Year bank holiday days, and is normally closed on Good Friday. Admission charge. Telephone 01522 528448.

A **commemorative plaque**, with a winged 'W' emblem and the motto 'Merit', carrying the inscription:

*In the hour of peril*
*people of Lincoln earned the gratitude*
*of the British nations*
*sustaining the valour of the*
*Royal Air Force*
*and fortifying the cause of freedom*
*by the gift of Spitfire aircraft*
*They shall mount up with wings*
*as eagles*

*Issued by the*
*Ministry of Aircraft Production 1941*

The plaque is believed to relate to Supermarine Spitfire V W3245 'Lincoln Imp'. Normally in store, the plaque formed part of an exhibition 'Wings over Lincolnshire' in 1994, which displayed aspects of early and military aviation in the county. It may form part of a permanent exhibition in the museum in the future. During 1995 the 50th anniversary of VE-Day is being commemorated by the museum, with a number of displays organised in conjunction with Lincolnshire Libraries.

In **Newport cemetery** (121/SK979725) off Newport north of the city centre is a Commonwealth War Graves Commission **cross of sacrifice**. The cemetery also contains a number of air force graves.

On the outside of the **North Lincolnshire College** building, on Park Street in the city centre (121/SK975713) is a **commemorative stone**, set high above a window on the Mint Lane side of the building noting that the Navy Army and Air Force Institutes (NAAFI) club was opened by HRH The Duke of Edinburgh KG KT on 11th December 1952.

Held by the **Royal Air Forces Association**, Lincoln branch, on Broadgate (121/SK978712) – the A15 – in the city is part of a propeller blade mounted on a base. This is the **Battle of Britain Memorial Golf Trophy**, first awarded in 1980, and presented to the winner of the annual junior golf contest organised by the Lincoln branch of the Royal Air Forces Association. The trophy is held by each winner in turn, and is not available for viewing except at the annual golf contest. The blade itself is believed to come from a Supermarine Seafire. A plaque, mounted on the blade itself, is inscribed:

*For the Young – In Memory of the Young*

In **St George's Hospital**, signposted on Long Leys Road (121/SK962731) west of the city centre, on Scampton Ward in the main hospital buildings is the **badge** of RAF Scampton, presented by the station in 1988. On Cranwell Ward are **photographs** of parades at the RAF College. On Burton Ward is a **print** of a Scottish Aviation Bulldog T.1 of the East Midlands Universities Air Squadron (originally presented to Saxilby Ward) and in the main reception is a large **print** of the Red Arrows flying over Britannia Royal Naval College, Dartmouth, Devon. Note that items in the wards can only be viewed by prior arrangement and that permission is not automatic.

In the headquarters of 204 (City of Lincoln) Squadron Air Training Corps at **Sabraon Barracks** (121/SK969730) on Burton Road (the B1398) north of the city centre is a **commemorative plaque**, with the badges of 50 and 61 Squadrons, together with the badge of 204 Squadron ATC. This was presented to the ATC unit when appointed honorary memorial guardians from 5th June 1994. There is also a **plaque** commemorating the opening of the headquarters on 11th March 1988 by the Mayor of Lincoln, Councillor Charles Ireland. The squadron also holds the original copy of the **warrant** authorising its formation in 1941. (Viewing by prior arrangement only.)

On **Steep Hill**, north of the city centre (121/SK976718) is the second **plaque** in Lincoln's heritage trail which commemorates the site were T E Lawrence ('Lawrence of Arabia') lodged in 1925 at the time he was serving at RAF Cranwell as Aircraftman Shaw.

## LUDFORD MAGNA
113/TF196890

In the **village centre**, on the A631, is a **memorial stone**, dedicated on 16th July 1978. It carries the badge of 101 Squadron along with the inscriptions:

*To Serve Was Their Highest Aim*

*This memorial is dedicated to the aircrews*
*of 101 Squadron Bomber Command*
*who failed to return from operational sorties*
*in the First and Second World Wars.*

*From 1943-1945 the Squadron was*
*based at Ludford Magna*
*where they made many friends.*

*A roll of honour is kept in the village church*

**No.101 Squadron's memorial stone in the village centre at Ludford Magna.**

In the **village church** (SS Mary and Peter – 113/TF201893), also on the A631, in the Lady Chapel, north transept, is kept the **roll of honour** of 101 Squadron, held in a display cabinet. Also here are the **standards** of 101 Squadron and of the 101 Squadron Association. The chapel also contains a photograph of a memorial to a 101 Squadron crew buried at Voué in France. Contact made with Voué in connection with this crew led to the two villages being officially twinned. Within the cover of the roll of honour is the badge of 101 Squadron and the unit's battle honours. Beneath is the handwritten inscription:

*These pages list the names*
*of but a few of those many who*
*'not afraid of any terror by night, nor for the*
*arrow that flieth by day,*
*fought the good fight, kept the faith and*
*finished their course'*
*That you may here stand in freedom,*
*unafraid, turning these pages of*
*their roll of honour*
*Arthur T Harris MRAF*

### MANBY (RAF)                          113/TF396870

On the technical/admin site of the former RAF Manby, now **Manby Park**, signposted off an unclassified road south of the B1200, in the former station headquarters building is a **memorial plaque**, with the logo of Anglian Water and the inscription:

*Guy Gibson Hall*
*Northern Area Office Lincoln Division*
*Anglian Water*
*Wing Commander Guy Gibson vc dso and*
*bar, dfc and bar,*
*was leader of the famous 617 'Dam Buster'*
*Squadron, which was formed in 1943 for the*
*specific task of breaching the Moehne and*
*Eder dams in Germany*
*This they achieved with the aid of the Barnes*
*Wallace bouncing 'bombs' and with*
*tremendous courage, on the night of*
*16th May 1943.*

The plaque is in the entrance hall, and also records that the offices were opened on 14th July 1983. Nearby are a **board** listing station commanders 1938-71, the **badge** of the College of Air Warfare, a **framed history** of RAF Manby, a **print** of a Lancaster, and **picture** of Wing Commander G P Gibson. Note that these items can only be viewed by prior arrangement, and permission is not automatic.

The offices of East Lindsey District Council are in the former College of Air Warfare building, now named Tedder Hall.

### MARTIN                                121/TF121599

At the **village church** (Holy Trinity) on the B1191, by the west window is a **memorial plaque**, dedicated on 13th September 1981, with the badge of 106 Squadron and inscription:

*To the glory of God*
*and in memory of the airmen*
*of 106 Squadron*
*who gave their lives in the*
*1939-45 war*

Nearby is a portion from a 156 Squadron Lancaster and the 106 Squadron **book of remembrance**. Outside the south door is a tree and a **plaque**, given by the Scoley and Wright families, remembering all who served at RAF Metheringham 1943-46.

### METHERINGHAM (RAF)                   121/TF109607

On the **former airfield** site, on an unclassified road (the former perimeter track) between the B1189 and the B1191 is a large brick **memorial**, in the style of a fireplace, with the badge of 106 Squadron. In the centre is the stone from the original 'grave' of 106 Squadron, carrying the unit's motto *Pro Libertate* ('For Freedom') and the dates 1917-19 and 1938-46. Set on the front are metal plaques. That on the left has the a map of the airfield, showing the position of the memorial itself, and that on the right has the inscription:

Part of Metheringham is still used for flying. North Kesteven Airfield Trail marker in the foreground.

*Metheringham, Syerston,*
*Finningley Coningsby*
*Dedicated to the airmen and airwomen of the*
*British Isles and Dominions, Europe and*
*America who served on and with 106*
*Squadron in World War Two 1939-1945*
*995 gave their lives*
*Lest We Forget*

The memorial was dedicated on 8th July 1992. Arranged in the gravel in front is a roundel design, and there is a mounting on the top for a (removable) model of a Lancaster. The badge of 106 Squadron on the memorial was made in Rottervalle in the Netherlands and presented by the Remembrance and Friendship Foundation, with whom the Squadron Association has had strong ties since 1980.

It has been suggested that the stone inset in the memorial is a replica. However, study of photographs of the 'grave' reveals distinctive aspects which support the conclusion that the stone is the original.

Above: **The impressive RAF Metheringham memorial, dedicated to 106 Squadron.**
Right: **Memorial to a 106 Squadron crew at the Metheringham Airfield Visitor Centre.**

Close by was a small **panel** giving details of the Salford Lancaster Memorial appeal (to commemorate the crew of Lancaster III PB304 'ZN-S' of 106 Squadron). This has now gone, as has a panel with a poem written by the memorial's builder.

A little further north of the 106 Squadron memorial (121/TF111615) is a **marker panel**, placed by North Kesteven District Council for its Airfield Trail. Adjoining the panel are two information boards – one with a site plan of the airfield and a map and details of the trail, and the other with details of a local countryside walk. There is another North Kesteven marker panel at 121/TF103606, on the B1189.

At **Westmoor Farm**, signposted on private road west of the B1189 at its northerly junction with the B1191 (121/TF101596) is the **Metheringham Airfield Visitor Centre**. The centre opened in October 1993, and is in located in the former ration store. Opening hours are April to October 10am to 5pm Saturday and Sunday and at other times by arrangement, telephone 01526 378270. There is a small shop, free car park. Admission free. It is planned to extend the facilities to include refreshments. The centre contains a detailed exhibition of the history of the station (including the 'funeral' of 106 Squadron), and a large model of the airfield and surrounding area with the dispersed sites.

In the centre is the **roll of honour** of 106 Squadron (the original was presented to the Bomber Command Museum in May 1993) which records the names of the 1,000 airmen who gave their lives on active service with 106 Squadron in the Second World War. Also here are **rolls of honour** for the Royal Australian Air Force, Royal Canadian Air Force and Royal New Zealand Air Force personnel of 106 Squadron, and that of RAF Metheringham, dedicated to all who were lost flying from the station.

There is also a **roll of personnel**, listing 106 Squadron's evaders and escapers. A **brick pillar** outside the entrance to the centre carries a propeller blade and reduction gear. This memorial was dedicated on 7th July 1993. The top of the pillar is an imaginative rendition of a Merlin engine, showing cylinder banks, exhaust stubs, and supercharger housing, all in bricks and tiling. The propeller unit was recovered from the Netherlands. A **plaque** reads:

*Memorial to*
*Squadron Leader F H Robertson & crew*
*Dedicated to the airmen of 106 Squadron*
*who were prisoners of war,*
*escapers, evaders and their aiders.*
*1940-1945*

A **memorial garden** is being established close to the centre. A **bench and plaque** keep the memory of Flight Lieutenant J Netherwood.

The centre regularly flies **flags and ensigns**, including those of Australia, Canada, the Netherlands, New Zealand, the Royal Air Force, and the Royal Canadian Air Force.

## MORTON HALL (RAF)     121/SK877641

On an unclassified road off the A46 is a **memorial plaque**, with the badge of 5 Group. **Morton Hall**, together with ancillary buildings, is now an HM Prison. The plaque was to have been displayed in the hall, but before it could be unveiled the hall was severely damaged by fire. The hall was subsequently demolished and the plaque is now mounted in the gate lodge. Note that the memorial can only be viewed by prior arrangement, and permission is not automatic. The memorial has the inscription:

*This plaque
was set in place as a tribute
to the men and women
of 5 Group Bomber Command;
to commemorate the sacrifices made by them
during World War II.
Morton Hall being the site of
the HQ of 5 Group
from November 1943 until
December 1945*

## MOULTON CHAPEL     131/TF293182

In the **village church** (St James), on the B1357, the **chancel screen** (dedicated in 1946) is in memory of Flying Officer A H M Clark.

## NAVENBY     121/SK989577

In the **village centre** on the A607 is the **Heritage Room**, which is open all year. Opening hours are 9am to 5.30pm Monday/Tuesday/Thursday/Friday and 9am to 12.30pm Wednesday and Saturday. There are exhibits on local history, including information on the RAF. There are also details of the North Kesteven District Council Airfield Trail.

Within the 'Lion and Royal' at Navenby is the Guy Gibson Room, commemorating the time when he lived there, as a Flight Lieutenant flying from Digby.

Opposite, the 'Lion and Royal' public house has the Guy Gibson Room, commemorating the period that Flight Lieutenant (later Wing Commander) G P Gibson lived there when stationed at nearby RAF Digby.

## NETTLEHAM     121/TF002756

In the headquarters of the **Lincolnshire Police**, signposted off the A46 is a **memorial plaque**, having a winged 'star and bar' badge with three Douglas C-47 Skytrains depicted. It is mounted in the main reception area, and is one of two presented by the 61st Troop Carrier Group before it left USAAF Barkston Heath in March 1945 (see also the Grantham entry). It is believed to have been previously mounted in the former Grantham police headquarters. Note that the plaque can only be viewed by prior arrangement and that permission is not automatic. The plaque carries the inscription:

*Sixty First Troop Carrier Group
United States Army Air Forces Barkston Heath,
Lincolnshire. 1944 - 1945
In appreciation of the fellowship,
hospitality, and understanding
shown by the constabulary of Lincolnshire
to all of us who, far from our own homes,
spent so many days in yours while we were
joined in destroying the tyrannical power
which threatened both
this testimonial is presented by
the officers and men of
the Sixty First Troop Carrier Group*

The **Nettleham Memorial Playing Field,** on an unclassified road near the village centre (121/TF010757) has a large **sign** recording the donation of the land in 1946 in memory of William Bailey and Flight Sergeant W Deburier of the RAF, and also to commemorate the service and sacrifice of the men and women of the parish in the Second World War.

## NEW WALTHAM      113/TA288061

At Peaks Farm on the A1098 is the **NATO Aircraft Museum** (formerly the Museum of Weapons Technology). The museum collection includes an English Electric Lightning T.5 and F.6, a Lockheed F-104G Starfighter and a SAAB A.35XD Draken. Opening hours are 10am to 5pm Tuesday to Saturday. Adjacent restaurant, toilets, car parking. Admission free. No telephone on site. **Lightning F.6** XR770 was given to the people of Grimsby by the Royal Air Force when RAF Binbrook closed in 1988.

## NORTH COTES      113/TA350006

In the **village church** (St Nicholas), on an unclassified road off the A1031, in the west window is a **stained glass panel**, depicting the badge of RAF North Coates (note the spelling) presented by the station in January 1971. The churchyard contains a number of air force graves. The **roll of honour** of RAF North Coates, previously displayed in the village church and later the station church is now in the council offices at Cleethorpes.

## NORTH KILLINGHOLME      113/TA144174

The **village church** (St Denys) is on an unclassified road north of the A160. On the wall of the south aisle is the badge of 550 Squadron, and a plaque inscribed:

*Presented to the people of
North Killingholme by
Wing Commander J J Bennett dfc and bar
founder & first commander
550 (Bomber) Squadron
A token of esteem and reciprocation
for the kindness & co-operation shown by
your people to the Squadron
January 1944 – October 1945*

A ***diplôme*** conferring a collective *Croix de Guerre*, and a certificate in English with the inscription:

**Above: Memorial to 550 Squadron, North Killingholme. Below: 550 Squadron badge inside the village church.**

*On June 6th 1944
the greatest liberating armada ever
assembled left the shores of England
For Bomber Command the invasion of
occupied Europe commenced the night before
At 23.34 hours Lancaster LL811,
squadron markings BQ-J
was the first aircraft in the first wave
to strike ahead of the main spearhead
by many hours, so setting
the momentous events in motion
That aircraft left from 550 Squadron, and this
historic operation put
North Killingholme on the map.*

*For the brave young lads of that crew and for
all their comrades who did not return
we dedicate this simple plaque.*

Close by the certificate is the **badge** of 550 Squadron and a photograph of 'B' Flight of the Squadron. The badge carries around its base the names of the crew (Flying Officer Bowen, Pilot Officer Zhomed, Warrant Officer Cleghorn, Warrant Officer Fyfe, Flight Sergeant Bodill, Sergeant R R Thompson, and Sergeant S G Thompson).

## NORTH KILLINGHOLME (RAF)      113/TA142175

On an unclassified road west of North Killingholme village, north of the A160, is a **memorial stone**, with the badge of 550 Squadron and the inscription:

*550 Bomber Squadron
Royal Air Force
3 January 1944
31 October 1945
Through Fire We Conquer*

The final line being the translation of the unit's motto *Per Ignem Vincimus*. Dedicated on 31st July 1982, the memorial is on Lancaster Approach, an access road to the former airfield site which is now an industrial estate (signposted). An inscription on the base records that it was donated by the North Killingholme Fittie Lands Charity.

## NORTH RAUCEBY
130/TF022475

At Heath Farm, signposted off the A17 is the **Cranwell Aviation Heritage Centre**. The centre is open all year, except for Christmas Day and New Year's Day. Opening hours: April to October 10am to 5pm daily and November to March 10am to 4pm daily (photographic exhibition only). The centre is operated by North Kesteven District Council and features an exhibition on the history of the RAF College, from its beginnings as the first military air academy in the world. There are details of the Council's Airfield Trail, and a Tourist Information Centre is staffed from April to the end of October. Toilets, free car park. Admission free. Telephone 01529 488490, Tourist Information Centre.

In the centre is a **commemorative certificate**, with the arms of the RAF College and the North Kesteven District Council noting that it was officially opened by Councillor Euan A Robertson, Chairman of North Kesteven District Council and Air Vice-Marshal David Cousins CB AFC, Air Officer Commanding and Commandant Royal Air Force College, Cranwell, on 8th June 1992.

## NORTHLANDS
122/TF334534

On **farmland**, off an unclassified road west of the A16 is a **stone cross**, with the inscription:

*Here lies the crew of a*
*Lancaster bomber which crashed on*
*29th January 1943*
*This memorial*
*is their families' tribute of love*
*and remembrance*

The aircraft, Avro Lancaster III ED503 of 9 Squadron, had been returning from a fighter affiliation exercise. The bodies of all the crew could not be recovered, and the ground was consecrated and the cross erected. The memorial is about half a mile north of the road, with access from a farm track. It is on private property, on actively farmed land and can only be viewed by arrangement, with permission

**Poignant stone cross and surround at the crash site of Avro Lancaster III ED503 of 9 Squadron, with the names of five on board who perished on 29th January 1943 and still lie there.**

obtained from Bishops Farm nearby. Care must be taken to avoid damaging crops. At the top of the cross a pilot's flying badge is inscribed, and around the base are low stone pillars with chains. On the reverse of the cross are inscribed the names of the crew: Donald A Brown, Charles W H Cocks, John Doran, Thomas S Henry, Bobby F Lind.

## NORTON DISNEY
121/SK890590

The **village church** (St Peter) is on an unclassified road between the A46 and A607. Inside is a **plaque** in memory of Flying Officer M Liniewski of 301 Squadron of the Polish Air Force. Also in the south aisle of the church is a **memorial plaque**, with the badges of 300 and 301 Squadrons and the inscription:

*Sacred to the memory*
*of the men of 300 & 301 Polish Squadrons of*
*the RAF operating from Swinderby,*
*who gave their lives for freedom 1939-1945*

*Za Nasza I Wasza Wolnosc*

The two squadrons were units of the Polish Air Force serving with the RAF. The Polish quotation ('For Our Freedom and Yours') dates back to the 19th century and a similarly worded declaration was on the doors of No 2 hangar at RAF Swinderby when the two units were there.

## RAUCEBY (RAF HOSPITAL)
130/TF041440

In the entrance hall of **Rauceby Hospital**, signposted just off the A153, is an **illuminated scroll**, with the badge of RAF Hospital Rauceby, badge of the Royal Air Force, arms of the City of Lincoln, Arms of Kesteven, and badge of the RAF Guinea Pig Club, commemorating the 50th anniversary of the RAF Hospital. The scroll records the history and work of Rauceby as an RAF Hospital from 1940-47. It was unveiled on 11th April 1990, and includes an illuminated poem entitled 'Fire'. The **badge** of RAF Hospital Rauceby, also presented on the 11th, is believed to be an unofficial design. It features the RAF roundel superimposed by the badge of the RAF Medical Services, and the motto 'Seeks New Fields'.

Note that these items can only be viewed by prior arrangement, and permission is not automatic. See also 'Late Additions' on page 70.

## REVESBY       122/TF298614

In the **village church** (St Lawrence), on the A155 is a **wooden panel** with badges of the Royal Navy, Army, and Royal Air Force and below a dedication to men of the parish who gave their lives in the Second World War. The panel is in the north aisle, and is also a memorial to the crew of Avro Lancaster III ND415 of 97 Squadron. The aircraft crashed on 23rd May 1944, following a collision involving Lancaster I LL967 of 57 Squadron, and this part is inscribed:

*Also of F/O W B Jardine*
*F/O G H Wright*
*F/Sgt A Dunae*
*Sgt J P Olive*
*F/O J W Paige*
*W/O R C W G Baker*

*Who were killed on operational duties*
*when their aeroplane crashed in this parish.*

## ROPSLEY       130/SK992342

In the **village church** (St Peter), on an unclassified road between the A52 and the B1176, is a **window of three lights** in memory of Sergeant Pilot W P Dales.

## RUSKINGTON       121/TF083511

In the **village church** (All Saints), on the B1188 is a **memorial plaque** to personnel of the 1st Airborne Reconnaissance Squadron, which took part in the Arnhem operation.

## SALTBY (RAF/USAAF)       130/SK858273

On an unclassified road between the A607 and the B676, is a **concrete badge**, depicting the trident symbol of St Volodyumyr. This badge

marks the use of the airfield site by Ukrainian prisoners of war, and is set in a grass bank at the side of the road. A modified version of the badge now adorns the tails of aircraft of Ukraine International Airlines, some of which can be seen visiting the UK. Although part of the former station site lies within Lincolnshire the badge itself is in Leicestershire.

## SANDY BANK       122/TF259551

In August 1994 a **white post** appeared in a field on **farmland** off an unclassified road between the B1183 and the B1192, and is believed to mark the crash site of a Lancaster of 83 Squadron from RAF Coningsby. A memorial service was held at the site, but it is not known if a permanent memorial is to be erected.

**Memorial to the crew of a 101 Squadron Lancaster at Scallows Hall.**

## SCALLOWS HALL       113/TF247948

In the grounds of **Scallows Hall**, off an unclassified road between the A18 and the B1203, in a field can be found a large **memorial cross**, with on the base the inscription, part of which has become weathered and difficult to read:

*Pray for the Souls of*
*F Oliver, W Reid, R Spierling, I W Anderson,*
*S G Burton, R S Bradbury, A D Wells*
*Air crash,*
*5th December 1943*

*Jesu mercy*
*Pray For Us*

The memorial is to the crew of Avro Lancaster III DV270 of 101 Squadron, and was dedicated in July 1948. Note that the memorial can only be viewed by prior arrangement, and permission is not automatic.

## SCAMPTON       121/SK948795

At the **village church** (St John Baptist), on the B1398, on the south wall of the nave is an RAF ensign, with below a **memorial plaque**, with the badge of RAF Scampton and the inscription:

*To mark the Diamond Jubilee*
*of the Royal Air Force*
*and the close association between*
*Royal Air Force Scampton*
*and this church*
*during the years*
*1917-1919 and 1936-1978*

There is also a **plaque** in memory of Flight Lieutenant P Stacey.

A **Royal Air Force Chapel** in the north aisle was dedicated on 12th February 1995. The altar and the pews were donated by RAF Scampton.

On the north wall of the chapel is the **badge** of the Burma Star Campaign, presented by RAF Asansol and Bishnupur on 16th May 1992. Below can be found a framed copy of the Kohima Epitaph:

*When you go home*
*Tell them of us and say*
*For your tomorrow*
*We gave our today*

It is understood that the station **honours and awards boards** will be mounted in the chapel on the closure of RAF Scampton.

A Commonwealth War Graves Commission **cross of sacrifice** stands in the churchyard, which contains a number of air force graves. It is understood that the **Hannah Rose** will be planted in the churchyard on the closure of RAF Scampton.

---

**RAF SCAMPTON**                  121/SK973792

Standing beside the A15, the closure of this famous station was announced in the government's defence costs study in July 1994. Headquarters Central Flying School moved to RAF Cranwell in May 1995, and the Red Arrows are to move to RAF Marham in October 1995.

Note that the Hannah Rose is by the main gate and car park, and may normally be viewed subject to operational requirements. All the other items on the station can only be viewed by prior arrangement, and such permission is not automatic.

The station currently keeps the **scroll** of the granting of the Freedom of the City of Lincoln to RAF Scampton on 14th May 1993.

A **memorial plaque** set into the ground between Nos 2 and 3 hangars, and with the inscription:

*On this spot Her Majesty Queen Elizabeth*
*The Queen Mother presented the standard to*
*No 617 Squadron when she visited this station*
*on 14th May 1959. The ceremony was*
*performed in brilliant sunshine in the presence*
*of many distinguished members of the*
*wartime squadron, including*
*Commonwealth members*

The standard presented by the Queen Mother is now laid up in Lincoln Cathedral, a second standard being presented to 617 Squadron in 1988.

In the headquarters of the **Central Flying School** a **memorial plaque**, with the arms of the CFS and the inscription:

*The Central Flying School Museum*
*opened by Her Majesty,*
*Queen Elizabeth*
*The Queen Mother*
*Commandant in Chief*
*Central Flying School*
*2 May 1985*

Also, the **Queen's Colour** for the Central Flying School. This current Colour was presented by the Queen Mother in June 1992, marking the 80th anniversary of the CFS.

The **Hannah Rose**, presented by the 83 Squadron Association in memory of Flight Sergeant J Hannah vc. The rose bed and **memorial plaque** are opposite the **guardroom**. There have been persistent reports of a **rose-bed** to commemorate those who undertook national service post-war, but no trace of this has been found.

Barrack and office blocks are named after holders of the Victoria Cross, some directly associated with the station : Cheshire, Gibson, Hannah, Learoyd, Manser, Nettleton, Trent.

Also at RAF Scampton are the station **honours and awards boards**, the **grave** of Wing Commander G P Gibson's dog 'Nigger' near No 2 hangar, and **Folland Gnat T.1** XR571 (8493M) outside the hangar of the Red Arrows. The airmen's club is named 'The Flying Bowman Club', alluding to the badge of RAF Scampton.

Closure of the station in 1996 will bring about the transfer of various items. It is understood that the scroll granting the Freedom of the City of Lincoln will transfer to the keeping of the Ministry of Defence. The CFS pieces were moved in May 1995 to RAF Cranwell. The 617 Squadron plaque will move to the unit's current home at RAF Lossiemouth. The Gnat is planned to go to RAF Marham. The Hannah Rose and station honours and awards boards will go to Scampton village church and the stone on the grave of 'Nigger' will be placed near the 617 Squadron Memorial at Woodhall Spa.

The Hannah Rose, shown here in the days when Lancaster NX611 guarded the gate at RAF Scampton. (The Lancaster is now displayed at East Kirkby.)

---

**SCOPWICK**                  121/TF069581

The **village church** (Holy Cross), is on the B1191. On the north wall of the nave is a copy of the poem *High Flight* by John Gillespie Magee (see page 15), together with notes on RAF Digby and the nearby war graves plot of the village burial ground.

In the **village burial ground,** signposted just off the B1188 (121/TF069582), is a Commonwealth War Graves Commission **cross of sacrifice** together with a number of air force graves, including that of Pilot Officer J G Magee of the Royal Canadian Air Force. A **stone plaque** commemorates where Flight Lieutenant J H M Offenberg was originally buried.

## SKEGNESS 122/TF571631

It is understood that a **three-bladed propeller** displayed in the **lifeboat station**, on the seafront, was recovered from a Handley Page Hampden which had crashed into the sea off Skegness. A **memorial plaque** to the aircraft's crew has been proposed.

## SKELLINGTHORPE 121/SK927717

Adjacent to the village **Community Centre**, signposted on an unclassified road between the A46 and the A57, is a **memorial plaque**. Dedicated on 2nd June 1991, it is set on a semi-circular base of coloured bricks in the form of an RAF roundel, and surrounded by a low wall. The plaque carries the badges of 50 and 61 Squadrons and the inscription:

**Included within the design of the Skellingthorpe village memorial is a flower bed and bricks in the colours of the RAF roundel.**

**Village sign and heritage room at Skellingthorpe.**

*Royal Air Force Skellingthorpe*
*My brief sweet life is over*
*My eyes no longer see*
*No Christmas trees*
*No summer walks*
*No pretty girls for me*
*I've got the chop – I've had it*
*My nightly Ops are done*
*Yet in another hundred years*
*I'll still be twenty one*

*R W Gilbert*

*This memorial*
*was erected by*
*the people of this parish*
*in grateful remembrance*
*of the airmen and women of the*
*Royal Air Force*
*and other Allied air forces*
*who served at*
*RAF Skellingthorpe*
*within this parish*
*1941-1945*

The community centre stands on the site of the former village railway station which closed in 1955. The **Skellingthorpe Heritage Room** is located in what was the former weighbridge office. The Heritage Room is open all year: April to October 10am to 5pm daily and November to March 10am to 4pm daily. Opened in June 1993, the Heritage Room displays a permanent exhibition relating to RAF Skellingthorpe. Panels of photographs and text cover 50 and 61 Squadrons, Flying Officer L T Manser vc, and the airfield itself (including layout plans). Car parking. Admission free. No telephone on site. Standing close by, the **village sign** incorporates a Lancaster on one face.

In **The Holt School** (121/SK921714), signposted on a unclassified road between the A46 and the A57, the **roll of honour** of 50 and 61 Squadrons, 1939-45, is held in a display cabinet. The cabinet also holds a copy of the roll of honour, which is available for viewing by visitors. Note that the memorial can only be viewed by prior arrangement.

## SKELLINGTHORPE (RAF)

The **Birchwood and Doddington Park estates** south west of the city centre of Lincoln are built on the site of the former RAF Skellingthorpe, and are on unclassified roads off the B1190. Many of the roads have the names of RAF airfields and stations.

Adjacent to the **Birchwood Community and Leisure Centre** (121/SK934697), on Birchwood Avenue, stands a **memorial stone**, with the badges of 50 and 61 Squadrons. On each side are inscribed the mottos of 50 Squadron and 61 Squadron ('From Defence to attack' and *Per Purum Tonantes* – 'Thundering through the Sky' respectively) and the airfields at which each was stationed. On the rear are the plan views of

**At the Birchwood Community Centre is the memorial to 50 and 61 Squadrons.**

a Handley Page Hampden, Avro Manchester and Avro Lancaster. Also inscribed on the face is the detail of the unveiling, which took place on 3rd June 1989, and on the rear is recorded the donation of the site by Lincoln City Council on behalf of the citizens of the City. Panels on the wall at the rear note the memorial's dedication and that it was erected by the 50 Squadron and 61 Squadron Memorial Committee. On the face is the inscription:

*To the memory of the air crews and ground staff who gave their lives whilst serving with No 50 Squadron and No 61 Squadron 5 Group, Bomber Command the Royal Air Force 2nd World War, 1939 to 1945*

*To live in the hearts of those we love is not to die*

*Stranger pause a while and pray for your tomorrow we gave our today*

The **local church** (SS Luke and Martin– 121/SK931697), is on Jasmin Road. In the entrance porch of the church is a **memorial bookcase**, with the badges of 50 and 61 Squadrons. This was presented by the 50/61 Squadrons Reunion Association in memory of comrades who served at RAF Skellingthorpe between 1941-45.

In the **Birchwood Community Park** (121/ SK929691) is a **memorial garden**, surrounding a preserved section of the main runway. Access is by footpath off Witchford Road or Elvington Road, or a (long) path off Pershore Way. Trees have been planted, and the area has been landscaped. A **memorial stone** was also erected in the garden, but sadly was vandalised within a few days. It now stands in the grounds of the nearby Manser School.

Further developments are being carried out in the community park. One of the former dispersal points and a shelter have been incorporated in extensions to the park at the south western side of the former airfield site. More recently a pond, with large stones at its edge,

**Unusually shaped memorial to RAF Skellingthorpe at the Manser School.**

has been established at the point of the actual main runway threshold (121/SK926688) adjoining Doddington Road at its junction with the A46.

The **Manser School**, on Woodfield Avenue (121/SK930692), stands on the line of the main runway, and has a number of items chronicling its name. A small **museum** was maintained, but is in temporary store in the light of demands for teaching space. It is understood that the various items will be placed in the museum at The Lawn Visitor Centre in Lincoln. Note, these item can only be viewed by prior arrangement, and permission is not automatic.

In the entrance hall is a **plaque** in memory of Flying Officer L T Manser vc, of 50 Squadron. Also a **memorial plaque**, with the Arms of Lincolnshire County Council and the inscription:

*Lincolnshire County Council*
*Manser School*
*Opened on 29th April 1981*
*by Cyril Manser Esq*
*brother of F/O Leslie T Manser vc RAFVR*
*This School is built on part of the former*
*Skellingthorpe Airfield and it was from here*
*that Flying Officer Manser to whom this*
*School is dedicated took off for his part in the*
*first thousand bomber raid.*

Outside the school is a **memorial stone** marking the site of RAF Skellingthorpe. The memorial is in the stylised shape of an aircraft, and stands on a grassy mound adjacent to the playground. The stone was originally sited in the Birchwood Community Park.

In the **Lancaster School**, on Jasmin Road (121/SK932696), is the badge of 50 Squadron presented by the unit in February 1975. Also a **commemorative certificate**, with the inscription:

*Lancaster C I School*
*Our School was opened in September 1974*
*when the name 'Lancaster' was chosen by the*
*parents. It was thought to be a suitable name*
*because the school stands on the site of*
*RAF Skellingthorpe from where bombers*
*flew throughout the Second World War.*

The badge and the certificate are mounted in the entrance hall of the school, together with a painting of Avro Lancaster 'ED222', 'VN-L' of 50 Squadron, by a local artist. Note these items can only be viewed by prior arrangement, and permission is not automatic.

In the **Health Centre**, on Jasmin Road (121/SK933696), is a **memorial plaque** noting that it is built on the line of the east-west runway. On the exterior of 'The Wild Life' public house, Birchwood Avenue (121/SK940704) is a memorial plaque noting that the pub stands just inside the main entrance of what was RAF station Skellingthorpe.

The **library** on Larchwood Crescent (121/SK932697) occasionally displays a site plan of RAF Skellingthorpe and other items, in conjunction with the Manser School.

Adjacent to the footpath from Skellingthorpe village (121/SK924702) to the west of the wood bounding the A46, North Kesteven District Council intends to erect for its Airfield Trail a **marker panel**. The panel will stand near the former bomb storage area. It is also planned to erect an information board with a site plan of the airfield, and a map and details of the trail.

## SOUTH CARLTON 121/SK951766

The **village church** (St John Baptist), is on an unclassified road off the B1398. The former airfield nearby was used during the Great War. The pulpit, dedicated in 1919, carries a **memorial plaque**, with the inscription:

*Praise God for the brave men of*
*South Carlton aerodrome who gave their lives*
*in our defence*

## SPALDING 131/TF250222

In the **parish church** (SS Mary and Nicholas), off the A1073 is a **memorial plaque** to personnel of the 3rd Battalion the Parachute Regiment. The **town cemetery** (131/TF250238) contains some air force graves.

**The plaque and model of the 'Stamford' Spitfire Mk IIB P8505 inside Stamford Town Hall.**

## STAMFORD

In the **town hall** (141/TF031070), on St Mary's Hill in the town centre. Inside the entrance hall is the **badge** of RAF Wittering, and a plaque recording that it was presented by the station in 1970. The entrance hall also has a number of other unit badges, including those of RAF Cottesmore, the Tri-National Tornado Training Establishment, 1 Initial Training School, and the RAF Regiment. With the exception of the badges in the entrance hall these items can only be viewed by prior arrangement, and permission is not automatic.

In the courtroom is a large framed **certificate**, with the badge of RAF Wittering and the inscription:

*Approximately*
*seven and a half years ago that is,*
*on the 18th day of October 1949,*
*the Mayor, Aldermen and Burgesses*
*of Stamford sent to*
*Royal Air Force, Wittering,*
*a message which expressed their pleasure*
*at being associated with the Officers and*
*Airmen of Wittering.*
*At the same time the Mayor, Aldermen*
*and Burgesses wished all persons at*
*Wittering pleasant lifelong memories*
*of the time the members of the*
*Royal Air Force spent in Stamford and*
*in the neighbourhood of Stamford.*

*This message was*
*and is greatly appreciated by all ranks*
*and the time has now come when we*
*would like to show reciprocation of these*
*feelings and our pleasure at the kind sense*
*of understanding and hospitality*
*which exists between the*
*Citizens of Stamford*
*and the Royal Air Force.*
*Accordingly in token of such feelings we ask*
*the Mayor to accept, on behalf of the*
*Borough of Stamford,*
*a copy of the Station Badge of*
*Royal Air Force Wittering.*

The certificate, dated 21st May 1957, is signed by the station commander on behalf of the officers and airmen of RAF Wittering. Also in the court-room is a series of **boards** recording the Mayors of Stamford and notable events, including the Honorary Freedom of the Borough conferred upon RAF Wittering on 1st July 1961.

In the committee room is a framed **certificate**, with a photograph of the 'Stamford' Spitfire. The certificate also notes the detail of the plaque presented to the town by the Ministry of Aircraft Production, and which is now held in the Mayor's Parlour. The certificate carries the inscription:

*The Stamford War Time Spitfire.*

*In 1940 Stamford decided to buy its own Spitfire*

*A marker board was put on our Central Cinema*
*The target to reach was £5,000,*
*which in 1940 was a lot of money*
*The collection boxes went into every shop, banks, public houses, all the local firms*
*We had whist drives and dances*

*We watched, with great interest, the marker on the board, until it had reached £5,000*

*Then later, our own Spitfire with the Stamford crest on its body flew low over the town in thanks for all our effort*

In the Mayor's Parlour the town regalia includes a copy of the **scroll,** dated 1st December 1960, recording the granting of the Freedom of Stamford to RAF Wittering. This illuminated scroll has upon the arms of Stamford, the badge of the Royal Air Force, the badge of RAF Wittering, the arms of the Central Flying School and the badges of 27 other units.

A **silver salver**, with the badge of RAF Wittering, presented by the station to Stamford on the occasion of the granting of the Freedom of the Borough on 1st July 1961. A **Battle of Britain Victory Sword** presented by RAF Wittering to the town on its 1,000th anniversary.

A **commemorative plaque**, with a winged 'W' emblem and the motto 'Merit', and the inscription:

*In the hour of peril*
*people of Stamford and district earned the gratitude of the British nations sustaining the valour of the Royal Air Force and fortifying the cause of freedom by the gift of Spitfire aircraft*

*They shall mount up with wings as eagles*

*Issued by the Ministry of Aircraft Production, 1941*

This plaque commemorates the presentation of Supermarine Spitfire IIB P8505. A **model** of P8505 as 'OU-H' of 266 Squadron, is displayed, with the dates 2nd May 1941 (when it was first taken on charge) and 12th June 1943 (when it was destroyed in a mid-air collision with P8915 over Shropshire). A **model** of a BAe Harrier GR.5, presented to the town by RAF Wittering on the 75th anniversary of the RAF in 1993. Other items on display in the Mayor's Parlour include a framed photograph of a Spitfire and Tornado, and the badge of the *Luftwaffen-musikkorps* 2, Karlsruhe.

In the south transept of **St George's church** (141/TF03207.1) is the **standard** of 100 Squadron, presented on 21st October 1955 and laid up on 20th October 1985.

---

**STICKFORD**                    122/TF351599

The **Allied Forces Military Museum** is just off the A16. The museum is developing displays of items on the air forces which operated from Lincolnshire. Opening hours are 9am to 4.30pm Monday to Friday. Saturday and Sunday by arrangement. Admission free. Telephone 01205 480317.

---

**STRUBBY (RAF)**                122/TF446805

At the **former main gate** of the airfield site, just off the B1373 is a **memorial stone**, erected by members of the Lincolnshire Military Preservation Society in 1992, in memory of those who served at Strubby during the Second World War. The memorial stands next to the former guardroom, now the society headquarters .

Elsewhere on the site the Lincolnshire Lightning Preservation Society keeps its **English Electric Lightning F.3** XP706 (8925M). The aircraft can only be viewed by prior arrangement, and permission is not automatic.

---

**STURGATE (RAF/USAF)**          121/SK873877

An exhibition of the history of the airfield is displayed in the **former watch tower**, now the headquarters of the Lincoln Aero Club. The building is off an unclassified road between the A631 and the B1241.

---

**SUTTON BRIDGE**                131/TF478212

**The Royal Air Force Memorial Chapel in the village church at Sutton Bridge.**

At the **village church** (St Matthew) on the A17, in the north aisle is the **Royal Air Force Memorial Chapel** SS Michael and Philip, dedicated on 29th March 1957. It commemorates Commonwealth and Allied airmen who gave their lives whilst serving at RAF Sutton Bridge in the Second World War and particularly those laid to rest in the military plot of the churchyard.

The altar frontal carries the **badges** of the Royal Air Force, Royal Australian Air Force, Royal Canadian Air Force, Royal New Zealand Air Force, Polish Air Force and a Czechoslovak Air Force flying badge. Above it is the wording 'Greater Love Have No Man Than This'.

In the chapel is the **roll of honour** of RAF Sutton Bridge, 1939-45. The roll of honour gives details of those initially interred in the churchyard. Some re-interments have taken place since the original burials, and some personnel were also buried elsewhere. Other items within the church are: an **RAF ensign**, a **flower stand** commemorating Sergeant A H Goddard and also his family and a family **memorial plaque**, which includes Sergeant J Bateman.

In the churchyard is a Commonwealth War Graves Commission **cross of sacrifice** and a number of air force graves.

## SUTTON BRIDGE (RAF)    131/TF482209

By the side of the A17, at the southern end of the bridge over the River Nene, is a **propeller blade** mounted on a brick base. Erected on 1st September 1993, the memorial overlooks the site of the former airfield, and was organised by the Fenland Aircraft Preservation Society. A **plaque** carries the inscription:

*This memorial is dedicated to all members of*
*the Royal Air Force of all nationalities*
*who served at RAF Sutton Bridge*
*from 1926 to 1958.*

## SWINDERBY (RAF)    121/SK885620

A **marker panel** for the North Kesteven District Council's Airfield Trail is being considered. An

**'Lest We Forget', the clock tower and plaque in Waddington village.**

information board with a site plan of the airfield, and a map and details of the trail may also be erected.

## WADDINGTON

In the **village centre**, just off the A607 (121/SK977642), is a **barrel clock** on a metal post, and **plaque** mounted on a low brick wall with the badges of 463 and 467 Squadrons. Dedicated on 10th May 1987, the clock is in memory of those members of the units who gave their lives while serving with 5 Group Bomber Command during the Second World War. It carries the wording 'Lest We Forget'.

Nearby is the **village church** (St Michael). The **foundation stone** records that the original church was destroyed by enemy action (an air attack on RAF Waddington in the early hours of 9th May 1941). The raid also devastated the NAAFI (what is now the Raven Club) on the station. The churchyard contains a number of air force graves.

The **village sign** (121/SK978643) depicts aspects of life in Waddington, with many references to the Royal Air Force. On its southern face are views of the village, a Royal Flying Corps cap badge, the badge of RAF Waddington, an Avro Lancaster, a Maurice Farman Shorthorn biplane, and the memorial clock and plaque to personnel of 463 and 467 Squadrons. On the northern side is a distant view of the village, with an Avro Vulcan flying over.

## RAF WADDINGTON    121/SK982649

Note all the items on the station (signposted on an unclassified road off the A607) can only be viewed by prior arrangement, and permission is not automatic. It is *sometimes* possible to enter the station access road subject to operational requirements.

Within the station are the **standard** of 8 Squadron and the **scroll** recording the granting of the Freedom of the City of Lincoln to RAF Waddington on 25th April 1959.

On the station access road, near the guardroom is a **memorial stone**, with the badge of 44 Squadron and the inscription:

*44 (Rhodesia) Squadron*
*Royal Air Force*
*in memory of*
*those who served*
*'We will remember them'*

The memorial was dedicated on 18th May 1986, an inscription on the base recording that it was erected by the 44 Squadron Association. To the rear of the memorial is **Avro Vulcan B.2** XM607 (8779M), which flew operations in the Falklands War, and a **commemorative plaque** with the inscription:

*Avro Vulcan B Mk 2 XM607*
*was dedicated*
*for display by*
*Air Vice Marshal D Parry-Evans cbe RAF*
*on the occasion of*
*his annual formal inspection*
*14 July 1983*

The aircraft carries the three bomb tallies for the attacks against Argentine forces in the Falkland Islands. A separate **plaque** records details of the BLACK BUCK operations.

Outside the **8 Squadron headquarters building** is a **memorial stone**, with the badge of the squadron and a plaque dedicating it to 'Absent Friends'. It was presented by the 8 Squadron Association and erected in 1991.

At the station headquarters building, a **memorial clock** is above the entrance. In the entrance hall is a memorial **plaque**, with the inscription:

*Commemorative clock*
*presented by*
*members of 463 & 467 Squadrons*
*Royal Australian Air Force 8th May 1975*
*in memory of comrades*
*who did not return during*
*World War II*

Adjacent to the plaque is the **badge** of RAF Waddington and a copy of the poem *Maximum Effort*. In nearby display cabinets are a range of **trophies and badges** presented to the station. The latter includes a **plaque** with the badge of the 48th Tactical Fighter Wing, the shapes of Great Britain and a General Dynamics F-111, and the inscription:

*48th Tactical Fighter Wing*
*RAF Lakenheath*
*310th Contingency Hospital*
*RAF Nocton Hall*
*To the men and women of*
*RAF Waddington*
*Thanks for your generous support*
*of our 150-bed aeromedical staging facility*
*Allies in action, prepared for desert storm*
*September 1990 – March 1991*

In the **operations block**'s foyer is a large **board** listing station commanders, honours and awards. On this is a framed panel with the **badges** of RAF Waddington, and 8, 9, 12, 21, 23, 27, 44, 49, 50, 51, 57, 61, 82, 83, 88, 97, 100, 101, 110, 142, 207, 420, 463, 467, and 617 Squadrons.

Above: **The 44 Squadron memorial, in the shadow of the Waddington Vulcan.** Below: **Near the 8 Squadron headquarters is the unit's 'Absent Friends' memorial.**

The former briefing room is now **The Nettleton Room**, and a portrait of Squadron Leader J Nettleton VC is on display outside together with a replica of his Victoria Cross.

A **plaque** on the door commemorates the naming and the opening of the room on 14th November 1993. Inside the room is the **roll of honour** of both 50 Squadron and 61 Squadron, 1939-45.

The **badge** of 61 Squadron is also mounted on a plaque, a duplicate of one mounted on a **memorial** to the crew of Avro Manchester I L7518, shot down on 26th March 1942. The people of Warmen Huizen in the Netherlands unveiled the memorial in March 1984 and the duplicate was presented to RAF Waddington. The **badges** of 463 and 467 Squadrons, with a plaque noting they were presented by the units in May 1975. The base on which the badges and plaque are mounted is in the shape of Australia.

Further items in the Nettleton Room: a Royal Air Force **ensign**; full size framed colour photographs of the **standards** of 44 and 50 Squadrons. **Boards** listing the commanding officers, honours and awards, aircraft and bases of 44 Squadron. Framed **badges** of 49, 61, 82, 83, 88, 97, 110, 142 Squadrons. In addition, there is the original (unofficial) **badge** of 503 Squadron. This displays the arms of the City of Lincoln, with an eagle above and the title 'County of Lincoln Bombing Squadron' on the scroll.

A framed **commemorative print** of Vulcan B.2 XM607 produced to mark the first BLACK BUCK bombing sortie in the Falklands War.

The room contains many other items associated with the Station, including photographs and details of squadrons resident over the years. There is a framed copy of the **programme** for the presentation of the standards of 44 and 50 Squadrons by HRH Princess Marina at RAF Waddington on 15th June 1967, the **badge** of RAF Waddington, and a number of other **ensigns**.

The **Raven Club** has in its entrance hall, a **memorial plaque**. Adjacent to the plaque is a photograph of the damaged building, and the appropriately named Phoenix Bar is on the first floor. The plaque carries the inscription:

*This club is named in memory of
Mrs Constance Raven,
a former manageress
who together with the following members
of her staff was killed by enemy action
on the night of
9th May 1941
Joan Bodinner, Frances Nacey,
Alice Brown, Elizabeth M Turner,
Marie Easton, Irene Woods*

*The club was opened by Mrs D C Stapleton
wife of the Air Officer Commanding
No 1 Group RAF
on 17th September 1964*

It is understood that there have been proposals for a **memorial** to personnel of 207 Squadron to be erected on the station. See also 'Late Additions' on page 70.

---

## WASHINGBOROUGH                    121/TF018705

In the **Washingborough Hall Country House Hotel** (on an unclassified road off the B1190) is a framed **certificate**, with the badge of 83 Squadron and the inscription:

*Ground Crew Register 1989 Reunion
at Washingborough Hall
Country House Hotel
May 16, 17 & 18th
Scampton – Wyton – Coningsby
1939 – 1945*

Nearby is the **village church** (St John). Eight windows in the clerestory commemorate an airship attack in 1916.

---

## WELLINGORE                        121/SK982566

On the A607 is the **Wellingore Heritage Room**, open all year. Opening hours are 9am to 5pm daily. The Heritage Room has an exhibition of local history, that for the Royal Air Force including details on RAF Coleby Grange, RAF Metheringham, and RAF Waddington.

---

## WELLINGORE (RAF)

On the north east and south west corners of the **former airfield site** are two **marker panels** placed by North Kesteven District Council for its Airfield Trail. One is on an unclassified road (Ermine Street), between the A15 and A607 at 121/SK994549. Adjoining the panel is an information board with a site plan of the airfield, and a map and details of the trail. The other is on an unclassified road, to the east of the A607 at 121/SK978542.

---

## WELTON                            121/TF012798

In the **village church** (St Mary), on an unclassified road between the A15 and A46, is a **memorial window** in the north aisle, with the inscription:

*To the Glory of God
and in honour of the Officers and Men of the
Royal Air Force who died in the service
of their Country.
'Their name liveth for evermore'*

The window of three main lights was erected in 1921, and commemorates the link with RAF Scampton. The **badges** of the Royal Naval Air Service, Royal Flying Corps, and Royal Air Force (and the Air Force Cross) are shown above a depiction of St Michael slaying the dragon of evil, and aircraft in flight in the skies above Lincoln Cathedral and the surrounding countryside. Above the pulpit is a Squadron Leader's **pennant.**

---

## WICKENBY (RAF)                     121/TF104810

At the entrance to **Wickenby airfield**, signposted on an unclassified road off the B1399 is a **memorial stone**, with the badges of 12 and 626 Squadrons. Dedicated on 6th September 1981, the memorial stands on part of the old perimeter track. A representation of Icarus falling is on the face. It carries the inscription:

*Royal Air Force Wickenby
No 1 Group Bomber Command
1942 — 1945*

*In memory of one thousand and eighty men
of 12 & 626 Squadrons
who gave their lives on operations
from this airfield
in the offensive against Germany
and the
liberation of occupied Europe*

*Per ardua ad astra*

**The Petwood Hotel, Woodhall Spa, officers' mess for the 'Dam Busters'.**

## WOODHALL SPA

The **Woodhall Spa Cottage Museum** is signposted just off the B1191 in the town centre (122/TF196633). The museum is open from Easter to September. Opening hours are 10am to 5pm Monday to Saturday and 11pm to 5pm Sunday.

The museum building, which also incorporates the Tourist Information Centre, was manufactured by Boulton and Paul. Admission charge for adults. Telephone 01526 353775.

The museum has a room dedicated to 617 Squadron. The permanent display was extended in 1993 to mark the 50th anniversary of the formation of the squadron, and includes information on RAF Woodhall Spa.

At the **Petwood Hotel** (122/TF193638), signposted off the B1191, is a **memorial plaque**, with the badge of 617 Squadron and an inscription noting that it was the officers' mess 1943-45. A large composite **painting** of the activities of 617 Squadron, is dedicated to the unit. The plaque and the painting are in the Squadron Bar, which houses a wide range of **memorabilia** primarily related to 617 Squadron. These include a large bough from a tree in the Soviet Union, which was struck by one of the squadron's Lancasters in 1944 during an operation to attack the German warship *Tirpitz*. The **badges** of Bomber Command and 617 Squadron are mounted in the reception, and in the car park is an example of one of the practice mines used in the weapon trials for the raid on the dams. The hotel regularly flies a Royal Air Force **ensign**.

In **Royal Square Gardens** (122/TF193631) at the junction of the B1191 and B1192 is the well-known, and huge, **memorial stone**, in the shape of a breached dam. It carries the badge of 617 Squadron and the inscriptions:

*They died for your freedom*
*This memorial commemorates the sacrifice of*
*204 aircrew of 617 'Dam Buster' Squadron RAF*
*in the Second World War 1939-1945*
*Erected by their comrades and dedicated*
*on the 17th May 1987*

Dominating the crossroads in the centre of Woodhall Spa, the impressive 617 Squadron 'Dam Buster' memorial.

*The Dams 1943*
*Fortress Europe 1943-44*
*Normandy 1944*
*Tirpitz 1944*
*Biscay Ports 1944*
*France and Germany 1944-45*
*German Ports 1945*
*Channel and North Sea 1944-45*
*617 Squadron*

The latter part lists the battle honours of 617 Squadron. The memorial carries the **roll of honour** inscribed in the spillways. The number of names originally carved was 201, the inscription was subsequently amended to include air gunners temporarily posted on to 617 Squadron to make up eight man crews for an operation, and the original figure may still be discerned.

Nearby is a **commemorative plaque** recording that the Woodhall Spa Royal Hotel originally stood on the site and was damaged by enemy action on the night of 17/18th August 1943. It is understood that the **stone** on the grave of Wing Commander G P Gibson's dog 'Nigger' will be placed near to the 617 Squadron memorial on the closure of RAF Scampton.

The **village church** (St Peter – 122/TF197632), is on the B1191. On the wall of the south aisle is a **memorial plaque**, with the badge of 619 Squadron and the inscription –

*This plaque was dedicated on*
*18th April 1993*
*to all who served in*
*619 Squadron RAF*
*1943 – 1945*

*'They came in the Defence of Freedom'*

At the west end of the nave is the **badge** of 617 Squadron. Outside the church is a **flagpole**, and a **plaque** stating that it was presented to St Peters by members of the 619 Squadron Association on 18th April 1993.

## RAF WOODHALL SPA 122/TF204611

To the south of Woodhall Spa village, signposted off the B1192, by the guardroom is a **three-bladed propeller** and centre hub mounted on a plinth, and a **plaque** on the dome of the propeller hub with the inscription: 'Over 50 years of dedicated service, Royal Air Force Woodhall Spa, 5th June 1993'. When the memorial was dedicated, the **badges** of 25, 97, 617, and 627 Squadrons were mounted on the plinth. Adjacent to the memorial was a **panel** inscribed:

*The Memorial*
*The Royal Air Force Woodhall Spa*
*memorial has been placed as a tribute to the*
*personnel who have served at this unit during*
*its 50 year existence*

*It also serves as a reminder of the many*
*servicemen and women who gave their lives*
*during World War Two*

The panel also gave details of the construction of the memorial, and it is believed that the panel and the squadron badges (and also the badge of 619 Squadron) will be displayed at services of remembrance. Note that this part of the airfield site comes under the control of RAF Coningsby. The memorial can only be viewed by prior arrangement, and permission is not automatic.

At the former No.1 communal site, on the B1192 (122/TF217596), is the **Thorpe Camp Visitor Centre**, being developed by the Thorpe Camp Preservation Group. The centre opened on 17th July 1994, and features a museum dedicated to RAF Woodhall Spa and its squadrons, and civilian life in Lincolnshire during the Second World War. Opening hours are May to October, Sunday and bank holidays 2pm to 5.30pm and at other times by arrangement. The indoor exhibition has displays on the station and individual squadrons, the Royal Observer Corps, and Airborne Forces in Lincolnshire. Larger items include one of the Royal Aircraft Establishment developed arrester gear units from the airfield. Fairchild Argus II G-AJOZ is stored. Refreshments, access and facilities for disabled people, toilets, free car park. Admission charge. No telephone on site.

The 627 Squadron **book of remembrance**, which was dedicated at Woodhall Spa church on 6th June 1993, is held in a display cabinet — a copy is available for viewing by visitors. Within the cover is the inscription:

*This book was compiled on the 50th*
*Anniversary of the formation of*
*No 627 Squadron, Royal Air Force,*
*to record and commemorate those members*
*who died whilst serving on the Squadron*
*23rd November 1943 to 30th September 1945*
*Oakington, Cambridgeshire and*
*Woodhall Spa, Lincolnshire.*
*They were our colleagues and friends.*

*We will remember them.*

**Display case holding the 627 Squadron book of remembrance at Thorpe Camp.**

**Rolls of honour** for other squadrons while they were resident at Woodhall Spa are being prepared: 97, 617, 619 and 627 Squadrons.

Outside the centre is a **plaque** in memory of Corporal A Mee, Women's Auxiliary Air Force.

Close by is 'The Blue Bell' public house, which has items relating to RAF Woodhall Spa and a propeller blade mounted outside the door.

## WRANGLE 122/TF425508

In the **village church** (SS Mary and Nicholas), off the A52, is a **memorial plaque**, with the badges of the United States 8th Air Force and the 392nd Bombardment Group and the inscription:

*To the glory of God*
*and in honoured memory of the crew*
*of B24 [sic] Liberator 42-95103*
*of 579th Bomb Sqn,*
*392nd Bomb Group of US Air Force.*
*Who lost their lives when their aircraft*
*crashed on Wrangle Common,*
*13th July 1944.*

*1st/Lt Norman J Hunt, T/Sgt Harold C*
*Wilkinson, 1st/Lt Peter B Roetzel,*
*S/Sgt W E Caurington, 2nd/Lt William J*
*Hession, S/Sgt Daniel L McEwan, T/Sgt Walter*
*L McKinzie Jnr,*
*S/Sgt Leonard A Jackson*

*RIP*

*S/Sgt Mark Osment was the sole survivor*

The plaque, mounted on the wall of the north aisle, carries a depiction of a Consolidated B-24 Liberator and also records that it was erected by the Lincolnshire Aircraft Recovery Group. The aircraft was from the 392nd Bombardment Group at USAAF Wendling. When the plaque was dedicated on 9th July 1994 an exhibition was mounted in the church, and the various items form part of a permanent display at the Lincolnshire Aviation Heritage Centre.

# ACROSS THE BORDER

This section deals with the significant memorials close to the Lincolnshire border.

**COTTESMORE,** Leics (Rutland)    130/SK902136

In the **village church** (St Nicholas), on the B668, can be found the **Air Forces Memorial Chapel**, dedicated in 1949. In the **village burial ground**, (130/SK906140, on an unclassified road off the B668) is a Commonwealth War Graves Commission **cross of sacrifice**, and a number of air force graves.

**RAF COTTESMORE,** Leics    130/SK913151

RAF Cottesmore is signposted off the B668. Outside the guardroom is a **plaque** in memory of the comradeship between the Royal Air Force and the United States Army Air Force. Note that the memorial can only be viewed by prior arrangement, and permission is not automatic.

**NEWARK,** Notts    121/SK805526

At the **Polish Air Force Cemetery** in the town cemetery, signposted on London Road (the A6065) south of the town centre, is the **Polish Air Force Memorial.** This was unveiled on 15th July 1941 by the President of the Republic of Poland.

Also here is the **Warsaw Air Bridge Memorial**, dedicated on 3rd October 1989. Close by is a Commonwealth War Graves Commission **cross of sacrifice**.

The cemetery contains the graves of over 300 personnel from the Polish Air Force, Polish Resettlement Corps, and Polish Parachute Brigade, as well as those of Commonwealth personnel.

On the outside of the **National Westminster Bank** in Stodman Street (121/SK798539), just off the market square, is a **plaque**, depicting a Lancaster and crew, dedicated to personnel who served on the nearby airfields during the Second World War. The plaque was unveiled on 4th June 1993.

In the churchyard of the **parish church** (St Mary Magdalene – 121/SK799539) in the town centre is a Commonwealth War Graves Commission **cross of sacrifice**.

**SPROXTON,** Leics    130/SK856244

In the **village hall**, on an unclassified road between the A607 and the B676, is a **memorial plaque** to personnel of the 62nd Troop Carrier Squadron of the 314th Troop Carrier Group from USAAF Saltby.

**Warsaw Air Bridge Memorial, Newark.**

**TINWELL,** Leics (Rutland)    141/TF006063

In the **village church** (All Saints), on the A6121, is a **memorial** to aircrew and paratroops who died in a collision between two Douglas C-47 Skytrains of the 315th Troop Carrier Group from USAAF Spanhoe Lodge, Northamptonshire, on 8th July 1944.

**WINTHORPE (RAF),** Notts    121/SK832562

The **Newark Air Museum**, signposted from the A1 and on an unclassified road between the A17 and the A46, is open daily all year, except for Christmas Eve, Christmas Day, and Boxing Day. Opening hours are April to October 10am to 5pm Monday to Friday; 10am to 6pm Saturday and Sunday and November to March 10am to 4pm daily. Visits at other times by arrangement.

An impressive and award winning collection of over 40 aircraft (including Avro Vulcan, Avro Shackleton, Gloster Javelin, DH Heron, and SAAB Draken). Some aircraft are occasionally opened (eg Vulcan, Hastings, Shackleton), but details should be checked in advance. Indoor displays include an aircraft exhibition hall, plus shop, refreshments, access and facilities for disabled people, toilets, free car park. Admission charge. Telephone 01636 707170.

Over the years there have been changes. Some memorials have been repositioned, others repaired or replaced. Some have simply gone.

The following lists the major changes over the years, and it will be appreciated that viewing of almost all those items which are in temporary store or held elsewhere will not normally be possible.

## No 460 SQUADRON RAAF TROPHY

The **Medium Bomber Efficiency Trophy** was presented to Bomber Command in 1955 on behalf of the 460 Squadron Association in memory of those personnel killed in the Second World War. The small figure of an angel with, below, the badge of 460 Squadron, flanked by wings. Behind, pillars support a large ring with the numerals '460' and the words 'Royal Australian Air Force Squadron'. On the base is inscribed:

*In remembrance of the*
*Squadron's thousand dead*

The trophy was first won by 90 Squadron in 1959 and is believed to have been last presented in 1981, to 617 Squadron when serving at RAF Scampton. By this time it had been renamed the Vulcan Efficiency Trophy.

## BARDNEY

The small **9 Squadron museum** adjacent to the squadron memorial has closed, and most of the items transferred to the Lincolnshire Aviation Heritage Centre at East Kirkby.

## BINBROOK (RAF)

The **scroll** recording the granting of the Freedom of Grimsby to the station on 1st April 1966 is now in the keeping of the Ministry of Defence. The **scroll** recording the granting of the Freedom of Grimsby to 12 Squadron on 11th September 1954 is with the unit at its new home of RAF Lossiemouth, Grampian. The **'grave'** whose headstone carried a warning to bomb aimers to carry out visual checks is believed to have gone many years ago. The former married quarters site is now known as Brookenby village.

## BOMBER COUNTY AVIATION MUSEUM

The museum, now at the former RAF Hemswell site, was previously at Cleethorpes and before that at Elsham Hall. It was originally known as the **Humberside Aviation Museum**.

## ELSHAM WOLDS (RAF)

The memorial stone dedicated in 1989 replaced a small **plaque**. This plaque, dedicated in 1981, is now held by the secretary of the Elsham Wolds Association and carries the inscription:

*RAF Elsham Wolds 1941-1945 No 1 Group*
*Bomber Command*
*103 Squadron*
*576 Squadron*
*This memorial was erected by*
*members of the Elsham Wolds Association in*
*proud and loving memory*
*of the men and women of the*
*RAF WAAF all Dominions and other*
*Allied air forces*
*who gave their lives whilst serving*
*at this Station.*

*That others might live in freedom.*
*They did not die in vain.*

## FALDINGWORTH (RAF/PAF)

A Polish **eagle set in gravel** on one of the 'B' Flight dispersals has now gone.

## FISKERTON (RAF)

With the closure of the Royal Observer Corps headquarters building the **plaque** marking the 50th anniversary of 15 Group is in safe keeping in the Lincoln area awaiting a permanent home. The plaque, unveiled on 6th September 1986, together with the badge of the Royal Observer Corps, has the inscription:

*To commemorate the 50th anniversary*
*of the Lincoln Group*
*Royal Observer Corps*

**The original plaque in the Elsham Wolds memorial garden.**

## GOXHILL (RAF/USAAF)

The **plaques** on the memorial have been replaced (see main text). The current location of the original plaques is not known. As with the current plaque it carried the badges of the USA and of the US 8th Air Force, and the depiction of the hands clasped in greeting (but not the P-38 Lightning). The text of the original main memorial plaque read:

> United States Army Air Force
> No 345 Base. Goxhill
> Fighter Training Group
> June 1942 – February 1945
>
> Gone, but not forgotten

The wording of one of the side plaques appears to be largely unchanged, but the original wording of the other was:

> The propeller blade on this tribute
> is from a P38 Lightning, which flew from this
> airbase and crashed on the 26th May 1944
> in the parish of Goxhill. It was recovered by the
> Humberside Aircraft Preservation Society
> in September 1983.
>
> It represents the high price our countries paid for
> freedom.

## GRANTHAM

In St Vincent's, the **5 Group Heritage Air Museum**, a memorial to all those who had served in 5 Group Bomber Command from 1937 to 1945 was housed at this former headquarters of 5 Group. Many of the contents are now held by the Grantham Museum.

## HEMSWELL (RAF)

The former officers' mess on Lancaster Green (opposite the 170 Squadron memorial) at Hemswell Cliff was the **Hemswell Cliff Hotel**. The hotel closed during the early part of 1994, but it is understood that it may reopen in the future as a conference centre. The hotel contained the Lancaster Bar and Canberra Suite, and displayed many photographs and paintings, including an original painting by a local artist of Wellington X JA451 'BH-J' of 300 Squadron.

Also displayed within the Hemswell Cliff Hotel was a framed **certificate**, with the badges of 300, 301, and 305 (Polish) Squadrons and the inscription:

> 300 Dywizjon Bombowy
> 'Ziemi Mazowieckiej'
> 301 Dywizjon Bombowy
> 'Ziemi Pomorskiej'
> 305 Dywizjon Bombowy
> 'Ziemi Wielkopolskiej'
> Polskie Siły Powietrzne
>
> 300, 301, and 305 bomber squadrons
> of the Polish Air Force
> operated from RAF Hemswell
> and its nearby satellite
> RAF Ingham during 1941-1944.
>
> Za nasza wolnosc i wasza

## KIRMINGTON

The **memorial plaque** to 166 Squadron in the village church is not the original.

## LINCOLN

A **memorial plaque** was in the Girls' High School (now the De Montfort University School of Applied Arts and Design) on Lindum Road, commemorating the school's senior French mistress and a 44 Squadron crew. All were killed when Hampden I AD983 crashed on the staff residence on 22nd July 1941.

A large **model** in bronze of an Avro Lancaster (with 'bouncing bomb') flying over a dam fashioned from mahogany mounted on a base of chestnut from Lincoln Cathedral, in tribute to 617 Squadron, was displayed in the Waterside Centre in the city centre. This was raffled for charity in 1994, but the current location unknown.

## LINCOLNSHIRE AVIATION MUSEUM

Located in the old station yard at Tattershall, the **Lincolnshire Aviation Museum** closed in 1985. Some items have transferred to the Thorpe Camp Visitor Centre at the RAF Woodhall Spa site (see main text). The Panton Wing building, in memory of Pilot Officer C W Panton, was dismantled when the museum closed.

## METHERINGHAM (RAF)

The stone inset in the 106 Squadron **memorial** was originally placed on the Squadron's 'grave'. When 106 Squadron was disbanded on 18th February 1946 a mock funeral was held to mark the event. A grave was dug on the airfield, a coffin (filled with a history of the squadron, photographs, and various personal effects such as cap badges) buried, and covered with the stone. A cross was placed at the head of the grave, with the unit's 'birth' (1917) and 'death' (1946) inscribed on it. For some years this stone was held at the Newark Air Museum and is now incorporated into the 106 Squadron memorial.

## NAVENBY

A **memorial plaque** to Flying Officer K A Stevenett was mounted on a tree at the crash site, near the village. The plaque was removed when the tree died some years ago.

## SANDTOFT (RAF)

The contents of the small **museum** were lost when the flying club building was destroyed by fire some years ago.

## SPITALGATE (RAF)

The **scroll** granting of the Freedom of Grantham to the station on 10th July 1952 is believed to be kept by the Ministry of Defence.

## STAMFORD

It is understood that a USAF **badge** was set in the wall of a building towards The Meadows, but this appears to have been moved.

## SWINDERBY (RAF)

There were a number of items held at RAF Swinderby before its closure in December 1993. These have been moved, some (for example the freedom scroll) to the Ministry of Defence and others to the RAF School of Recruit Training's new home at RAF Halton, Buckinghamshire.

For some years **Canberra PR. 7** WT520 (8184M) stood near the hangars, but it was scrapped in 1991. Close to the aircraft were two plaques, both now in the keeping of Newark Air Museum. One gave details of the type, and the other the inscription:

The 106 Squadron 'grave' during the 'ceremonies' to disband the unit at Metheringham, February 1946. The stone used to cover the 'grave' now forms part of the squadron memorial.
Peter Green collection

*WT520 Canberra PR7*
*Dedicated to past and present members of*
*31 Squadron Royal Air Force*
*on the*
*occasion of the Squadron's*
*70th anniversary*
*and 30th anniversary*
*of the re-formation of 31 Squadron*
*in Germany with Canberra PR.7 aircraft*
*at RAF Laarbruch.*

*Refurbished at RAF Swinderby – Sept/Oct 1985*
*by members of 31 Squadron*
*RAF Association, 1406 Sqn ATC*
*and personnel of RAF Swinderby*

An **AK47 assault rifle**, and a **plaque** on the wooden stock with the inscription:

*Operation granby / desert storm*

*Presented to RAF Swinderby by*
*Sqn Ldr Steve Williams and Flt Lt Hugh Milroy*
*to mark the safe return of*
*all RAF Swinderby personnel*
*from the Gulf War*
*May 1991*

A **commemorative poignard**, and plaque with a crown and eagle, inscribed:

*Royal Air Force Benevolent Fund*
*Battle of Britain poignard*
*awarded to Royal Air Force Swinderby*
*for outstanding support 1978-1981*

A **Battle of Britain Victory Sword**, and plaque with an RAF roundel and the inscription:

*Battle of Britain*
*August 8th – September 15th 1940*
*Never in the field of human conflict was so*
*much owed by so many to so few*
*Winston Churchill,*
*House of Commons*
*20th Aug 1940*

The **scroll** recording the granting of the Freedom of Newark to RAF Swinderby on 8th April 1991. A framed **certificate**, with the badges of 300 and 301 Squadrons, and the inscription:

*300 Dywizjon Bombowy*
*'Ziemi Mazowieckiej'*

*301 Dywizjon Bombowy*
*'Ziemi Pomorskiej'*
*Polskie Siły Powietrzne*
*Krolewskie Siły Powietrzne*

*300 and 301 bomber Squadrons of the Polish*
*Air Force were the first units to be based at*
*RAF Swinderby when it opened in August 1940.*
*In January of the following year*
*the Squadrons were inspected by*
*His Majesty the King, and on 16 July 1941 the*
*Polish Air Force Standard was presented*
*at a ceremony held on the Station.*
*The Standard had been smuggled out of*
*occupied Poland, and was finally returned to*
*Warsaw in September 1992.*

*Za nasza wolnosc i wasza*
*For our freedom and yours*

A **commemorative sword**, and plaque with the inscription:

*The Wilkinson Sword of Peace*
*for 1985*
*Presented to Royal Air Force Swinderby*

The doors of No 2 Hangar at Swinderby, an impressive 'monument' to the Polish units 300 and 301 Squadrons. The doors were overpainted upon their departure in 1941.

The **barrack blocks** were named after holders of the Victoria Cross (Barton, Cheshire, Gibson, Lord and Reid), with a plaque in each recording the circumstances of the award.

**Training trophies** previously on the station included The Lincoln Trophy and The Halifax Trophy.

A large **Polish Air Force 'chequerboard'** and Polish eagle were painted on the doors of No 2 hangar. They were overpainted after 300 and 301 Squadrons left in 1941. They carried the inscription:

*Za Nasza Wolnosc I Wasza*
*For our freedom and yours*

## RAF WADDINGTON

When 1339 Wing Royal Auxiliary Air Force disbanded in early 1994 its **Oerlikon anti-aircraft guns** were put up for disposal. The guns had been captured from Argentine forces in the Falkland Islands, and were individually named after locations in the Falklands War (for example Mount Longdon).

## GATE GUARDS

There have been a number of changes over the years. At **Binbrook Lightning F.3** XP748 (8446M) and **Spitfire F.22** PK664 (7759M) stood by the main gate. The Lightning moved out in June 1988 for use as a range target and the Spitfire went to RAF St Athan, Glamorgan, in November 1988 for storage

**Vampire T.11** 'XD429' (XD542/7604M) was replaced at **Cranwell** by Jet Provost T.5A XW353 (9090M) in 1991. The Vampire moved to Edzell in Tayside.

**Meteor T.7** WH166 (8052M) left the gate at **Digby** for a private collection near Hereford in 1991. It was replaced by the replica Spitfire IX 'MJ832' (BAPC.229).

It is understood that the main gate of what is now **Rapier Barracks** (the former RAF Kirton in Lindsey) used to sport a pair of **BAe Rapier** surface-to-air missiles, but these have now gone.

**Lancaster I** R5868 (7325M) which stood by the guardroom at **Scampton** is now in the RAF Museum at Hendon. Its replacement, **Lancaster VII** NX611 (8375M) is now on display at the Lincolnshire Aviation Heritage Centre.

Both **Vampire T.11** XD506 (7983M) and **Lightning F.1** XG329 (8050M) have now gone from **Swinderby**. The Lightning is to be found at the Norfolk & Suffolk Aviation Museum, Flixton, Suffolk.

**Victor K.2** XL189 (8912M) which stood behind Vulcan B.2 XM607 (8779M) at **Waddington** near the main gate was scrapped in September 1989.

Above: **Avro Lancaster VII NX611 on duty at Scampton's gate; it is now on show at East Kirkby.**
Below: **Handley Page Victor K.2 XL189 was displayed with Avro Vulcan B.2 XM607 at Waddington. The Victor was scrapped in September 1989.** Alan Curry

Not every one of the memorials is exactly what it says. Apart from any obvious local spellings or layouts, some more fundamental points may also be recognised. Amongst them are the following, numbers in brackets relate to page references in the main text:

■ The reference to **RAF Dunholme Lodge** on the panel outside the William Farr School is not entirely accurate, as the school is built on part of the former station site, rather than the airfield itself. The wording of the board in the hall is better. (28)

■ The industrial estate built on the former **RAF Elsham Wolds** site is named, or at least signposted as, the Elsham Wold Industrial Estate. (31)

■ In **Fulbeck village**, the plaque carries the dates 1942-45 but the 931st Air Refueling Group was not formed at that point, and the United States Air Force was at that time the United States Army Air Force. The link is believed to be the 440th Troop Carrier Group of the US 9th Air Force which was stationed at USAAF Fulbeck. (32)

■ The dates on the plaque in St Vincent's at **Grantham** do not give the actual dates that the building was used as the 5 Group headquarters, which were October 1937 to November 1943. From December 1943 it was the headquarters of 9th Troop Carrier Command USAAF, and later the headquarters of 7 Group, Bomber Command. (33)

■ The inscription in the roll of honour of 207 Squadron in the village church, **Great Steeping**, differs from the detail on the memorial plaque also in the church. (33)

■ The Avro Lincoln depicted on the sign of the public house of the same name at **Hemswell Cliff** does not appear like one which ever graced the skies over RAF Hemswell, and its all silver scheme looks more like that of the Lincoln Mk 30s of the Royal Australian Air Force. (36)

■ The memorial books in **Lincoln Cathedral** cover a wider geographic area than is suggested by the inscription on the casket. Although some stations of 7 Group were in the county, others in that and other groups were as far apart as Lossiemouth in Scotland and Pershore in Worcestershire. The inscriptions in the books themselves are more certain. (40)

Exactly why (and when) the training groups were commemorated in Lincoln is not

**Suddenly Elsham Wold is singular, yet it was RAF Elsham Wolds.**

known, although it is right that personnel from the OTUs should be remembered and there are links with 1 Group and 5 Group in Lincolnshire. The books in the Cathedral are part of the total commemoration of Bomber Command, with the books of remembrance of 2, 3, 8, and 100 Groups in Ely Cathedral, and the book of remembrance in York Minster which commemorates personnel from 4 Group as well as those from 6 (RCAF) Group.

■ It is believed that the Wickenby Trophy at **Lincoln Christ's Hospital School** should depict Lancaster I ME758, 'PH-N' of 12 Squadron, which flew over 100 operations. ME756 was never operated by 12 Squadron. (41)

■ The plaque commemorating the **'Saracen's Head'** in **Lincoln** is fixed to a new structure, whilst the original building itself lies a few feet away to the north. Although the wording is accurate for where it is mounted, it is not clear why the plaque was not placed on the actual 'Saracen's Head' building. The original location of the canopy over the entrance to the former hotel can be made out in the balustrade over the shop frontages. (42)

■ The station headquarters building on the former **RAF Manby** site is now Guy Gibson Hall, offices of the Anglian Water Authority. Was Wing Commander Gibson ever stationed there, and why — apart from the obvious — should a water authority wish to commemorate 617 Squadron in this way? It is unfortunate that the spelling mistake should appear on the plaque. (44)

■ The name of **RAF North Coates** is of interest. The title was taken from the nearby village, but it appears that local pressure over the name brought about an official change of the village name in 1994 to the apparently more correct spelling North Cotes (47). A similar confusion exists with Halton Holegate, or is it Halton Holgate? (35)

■ Not all the airfield road names on the Doddington Park estate on the former **RAF Skellingthorpe** site are those of 1 Group or 5 Group. Langer Close should be Langar Close. (52)

■ The serial of the Lancaster in the painting at the Lancaster School on the former **RAF Skellingthorpe** site is not that of a Lancaster, but of an Airspeed Oxford. (53)

■ The debate is occasionally joined as to the unofficial title of **617 Squadron**. Should it be Dambusters or Dam Busters, and is it plural or singular? The style on the squadron's memorial at Woodhall Spa probably conveys the definitive answer – 617 'Dam Buster' Squadron, and thus The Dam Busters. (58)

Top: **Not all of the airfield road names on the Doddington Park estate, on the former RAF Skellingthorpe, are from 1 Group or 5 Group. Kirmington is fine ...**
Bottom: **...as is Langar, if it was spelt correctly.**
Right: **The 'Saracen's Head' in Lincoln, alas no more. A plaque marks its presence, but the plaque is mounted on the new building that replaced Woolworth's in this 1952 view.**
Lincolnshire Echo

# APPENDICES

## COLOURS AND STANDARDS OF THE RAF

In 1943, on the 25th anniversary of the formation of the RAF, King George VI announced his intention of awarding standards to operational squadrons and later announced the award of a Sovereign's Colour to certain formations.

Standards rank second to colours and show the squadron's badge, with scroll panels recording battle honours awarded to the squadron. Squadrons qualify for the award of a standard after 25 years service, or as a mark of the Sovereign's appreciation for especially outstanding operations. These banners are an outward sign of unity, loyalty and achievement, representing the spirit of the unit or formation, and honour those who have died in the service of their country. Each holds a special place, also representing the trust which the Sovereign places in the RAF.

Those in Lincolnshire include the first colour presented to the RAF, the King's (now the Queen's) Colour for the Royal Air Force College. This is displayed in College Hall, on the instructions of the late King, at all times when the cadets are in residence (being moved for the period of each recess) and is the only Sovereign's Colour of the armed forces of the United Kingdom to be on open display.

Those squadrons with a standard maintain it, as with colours, under strictly laid down conditions. Where a new colour or standard has been presented, the old one may be laid up at a nearby church (for example, those for 5 Squadron and for 11 Squadron are in the village church at Binbrook) or RAF station (the old colours for the RAF College are laid up in the College Church and a number of squadron standards are held in College Hall).

The RAF has been awarded over 100 battle honours, in a similar system to that operated by the British Army. The earliest battle honours are from the Great War, for example Western Front 1914-1918, and the latest is Gulf 1991. Previous rules permitted up to a maximum of eight battle honours granted in the two world wars to be emblazoned on a standard (those of the interwar period are not displayed). A decision in 1994 by the Air Force Board now allows a maximum of 15 battle honours to be displayed. However, this extension only affects South Atlantic 1982, Gulf 1991, and those battle honours which may be awarded in the future with the right of emblazonment. Squadrons with more than eight battle honours from the two world wars may not add them to their standards.

Local branches of the Royal Air Forces Association and the Aircrew Association also hold standards, as does the Polish Air Force Association, and the Royal Observer Corps Association (the local standard actually being the former standard of 15 Group ROC), and squadrons of the Air Training Corps have their banners.

A number of current and old colours and standards are held in the county and these are listed in the main text.

## AIR FORCE HERALDRY

The colours, standards, and badges of the air forces of the world have their common roots in the wider conventions of heraldry, and its purpose of identification. Within the air forces it has the additional function of inspiring loyalty, as well as displaying allegiance (particularly in the case of the RAF and Commonwealth air forces) to the Crown.

There are a number of excellent works on the subject, but the following is a note of some of the key aspects as they relate to the RAF.

**Badge:** Although in use since 1918, the badge of the RAF was not officially described until 15th September 1949.

**Motto:** *Per Ardua Ad Astra* was approved for the Royal Flying Corps on 15th March 1913, and was later adopted by the RAF. There is no authoritative translation.

**Ensign:** The RAF Ensign was introduced in December 1920. During the ceremonial on hoisting a trumpeter sounds *Attention*, followed by *General Salute*. On hauling down the trumpeter plays the *Retreat* (interestingly, this is played by the Chime of the RAF College). It is now the usual practice for a whistle to be sounded.

**Crown:** The crown displayed on RAF badges was originally the Tudor Crown, and on the accession of the Queen it was changed to the St Edward's Crown. These are normally referred to as either a 'King's Crown' or 'Queen's Crown' respectively. It is interesting to note the crowns displayed on the memorials. Some are engraved with squadron badges which bear the Queen's Crown and others the earlier King's Crown. For the period of the Second World War the correct device is that latter, but occasionally the current crown adorns the badge of a unit which disbanded before the Queen took the throne (for example, on the badge of the 550 Squadron memorial on the former RAF North Killingholme site). The situation is further complicated where a squadron is still operational. For example, 100 Squadron is currently at RAF Finningley, South Yorkshire, (although will move shortly with the planned closure of the station). The squadron memorial on the former RAF Grimsby site commemorates the period 1942-45, and the squadron badge on the memorial correctly displays the King's Crown.

**The 50 Squadron standard at RAF Waddington on the announcement of the award of the 'South Atlantic 1982' battle honour.**

**Squadron/Unit Badges:** Although the RAF had been using various badges since its formation it was not until 1935 that an Inspector of RAF Badges was appointed. The inspector, a member of the College of Arms, controls the preparation of any new badge before submission to the Sovereign for formal approval. Over 1,000 badges have now been approved. The basic frame of the circlet, surmounted by the crown, was introduced by the Inspector of RAF Badges. The scroll bears the unit motto, although a few badges do not have a scroll/motto. The pictorial component of the badge is intended to display the location of the unit, a local link, or a representation of its role or history. Local examples include the stylised representation of the Roman road and the runway extension on the badge of RAF Scampton, and the Lincoln Imp on that of 61 Squadron. A great many unit badges are current in Lincolnshire. One badge,

that of the Battle of Britain Memorial Flight, is particularly well known both in and outside the county. Despite this widespread use it is believed that this particular badge is in fact unofficial. Another badge, not so widely seen, is that of 619 Squadron. That too is unofficial, the design being submitted for approval as the squadron disbanded.

**Arms:** Arms have been granted to units in Lincolnshire. These include the RAF College, the College of Air Warfare and the RAF Central Flying School.

**Battle of Britain:** The Battle of Britain is the most distinguished battle honour of the RAF, and is commemorated annually. The Air Council decided in 1945 that 15th September should be known as Battle of Britain Day, and be observed annually with appropriate parades.

From 1946 there was to be a Battle of Britain Week, extending over the week which included 15th September. 'At Homes' would be organised at RAF stations on the Saturday, with services of thanksgiving on the Sunday (although the first Battle of Britain Sunday was held on 16th September 1945).

**Display Teams:** The RAF Aerobatic Team, the Red Arrows, needs little introduction. Other teams resident in Lincolnshire have included the Vintage Pair, the Poachers, the Macaws, and the Vulcan Display Flight.

## COMMONWEALTH WAR GRAVES COMMISSION

A notable feature of cemeteries in Lincolnshire is the number of Commonwealth War Graves Commission (CWGC) headstones marking service graves.

Until the Great War of 1914-18 (although more properly, the War of 1914-21 if the fighting involving the aftermath of the revolutions within Russia in 1917 is included) there was no official war body responsible for the British war dead. The individual efforts of Fabian Ware (later Major General Sir Fabian Ware) in recording burials on the western front in addition to his duties with a British Red Cross unit led to the formation of a Graves Registration Commission in 1915.

With the massive increase in casualties of British and Dominion personnel the Imperial War Graves Commission (IWGC) was created under Royal Charter in 1917. The IWGC became the Commonwealth War Graves Commission in 1960. The Commission was the first organisation given the duty of care of all the dead of a nation in any war. Its duties are to mark and maintain the graves of those killed, to build and maintain memorials to those who have no known grave, and to keep detailed registers.

One of the guiding principles was that each of the dead should be commemorated individually by name – either on a headstone or on a memorial – and that the headstones should be uniform, and make no distinction on account of military or civil rank.

Headstones of a design acceptable to all religions were agreed upon, inscribed with the regimental badge or national emblem, and also a religious emblem — either the Christian Cross or the Jewish Star of David. This was replaced by the Victoria Cross or George Cross where the recipient had been awarded either decoration.

Each inscription was to include the name, rank, regiment or unit, date of death, and also a short inscription provided by the next of kin if desired. The headstones are two feet eight inches in height, being referred to by the Commission as markers. Even within the CWGC there have been a number of slightly differing designs, and the following variations may be noted – the Great War, inter-war period, the Second World War (Commonwealth Polish, Czechoslovakian, German forces), post-war UK forces.

For large cemeteries a stone of remembrance was placed. This was designed by Sir Edwin Lutyens, engraved with the words 'Their name liveth for evermore'. This quotation, from Ecclesiasticus, was chosen by Rudyard Kipling. All CWGC cemeteries and plots of more than 40 graves have the cross of sacrifice, set upon an octagonal base and bearing a symbolic sword on its face. The cross was designed by Reginald Blomfield. Within Lincolnshire there are eight crosses of sacrifice and one stone of remembrance, and these are listed in the main text.

Between the world wars it was practice for serving airmen to be buried in the village cemetery near to their home, the headstone usually to a private design. Only the standard CWGC headstone was permitted as a grave marker overseas, and the Commission pressed for a similar system to be adopted for those who died within the United Kingdom.

In 1941 it was confirmed that next of kin could elect to make their own arrangements, and so a number of graves in village cemeteries are marked with private memorials or headstones. In the summer of 1943 RAF regional cemeteries were established. These enabled burials to be centralised, particularly those of Commonwealth personnel.

The CWGC regards war cemeteries as being any site with its own entrance, being walled or fenced. An extension to a civil cemetery or plot is also deemed a war cemetery if it has an entrance or wall/fence. Otherwise, burial sites are considered as war graves plots.

In Lincolnshire there are some 1,700 CWGC marked graves of the Second World War, of which 900 are those of air force personnel. The Polish Air Force Cemetery was established in neighbouring Newark. This contains over 300 graves of Polish personnel, together with graves of other personnel from the Commonwealth.

Scopwick burial ground contains an example of many of the CWGC headstone designs, together with a cross of sacrifice. Buried in this plot is John Gillespie Magee, author of the celebrated poem *High Flight*, who was killed flying from RAF Wellingore.

In the early 1960s most German graves in the UK not already in CWGC cemeteries or plots were transferred to the German Military Cemetery at Cannock Chase in Staffordshire, maintained by the CWGC. Local villagers were given an opportunity to decide whether to transfer German burials from their own cemetery, many in Lincolnshire choosing not to do so.

Nothing came of proposals to build joint memorials with the Allied nations, but there

**Their name liveth for evermore.**

remained the question of Allied war graves in the UK. The graves of other nationals who had died fighting under the Union Flag were to be treated as the Imperial forces, but the relevant governments had to be consulted about the treatment of the graves of independent Allied units.

Difficulties arose in 1945 with regard to Polish personnel, the IWGC being uncertain as to whether the Polish government (by then in exile) or the 'Government of National Unity' in Warsaw was responsible for Polish graves. In the end the Commission itself selected a distinctive headstone design, proceeded to mark the graves and undertook their maintenance, the British government meeting the costs in the UK.

A total of 1,700,000 men and women of the Commonwealth forces died in the two world wars. Of these, over 900,000 are commemorated on headstones over their identified graves and the remainder, who have no known grave, are commemorated on memorials. Perhaps the most well known national memorial for personnel of the Commonwealth air forces is that at Runnymede.

There are war graves in 145 different countries, mostly in the CWGC's 2,500 war cemeteries and plots, but many also in war graves in civil cemeteries and churchyards throughout the world. The records held at the CWGC head office in Maidenhead enable staff to help enquiries locate a particular grave or name on a memorial.

Almost all the war cemeteries and memorials are maintained by the Commission's own staff, although in a number of countries special arrangements exist. Those countries carry out care and maintenance on the CWGC's behalf. Care of war graves in cemeteries and churchyards is mostly entrusted to local and church authorities who maintain them in agreement with the CWGC.

In the UK only 5,000 are buried in Commission cemeteries. About 40,000 are buried in military plots in civil cemeteries, but over 120,000 graves are scattered in more than 12,000 burial grounds. Of all these some 30,000 are RAF and Commonwealth airmen.

## FURTHER READING

The following represent an excellent selection and are well recommended to the student of military and naval aviation in Lincolnshire.

*The Airfields of Lincolnshire since 1912*:
   R N E Blake, M Hodgson, W J Taylor;
   Midland Counties Publications, 1984.
*Aviation Landmarks*: J Gardner;
   Battle of Britain Prints International, 1990.
*Battle of Britain Memorial Flight*: W J Taylor;
   Midland Publishing, 1995.
*Bomber County, A History of the Royal Air Force in Lincolnshire*: T N Hancock;
   Lincolnshire County Council, 1978.
*Bomber County 2*: T N Hancock;
   Lincolnshire County Council, 1985.
*Britain's Aviation Memorials & Mementoes*:
   D J Smith; Patrick Stephens, 1992.
*The Buildings of England – Lincolnshire*:
   N Pevsner, J Harris, N Antram;
   Penguin, 1989.
*Courage Remembered, The Story Behind the Construction and Maintenance of the Commonwealth's Military Cemeteries and Memorials of the Wars of 1914-1918 and 1939-1945*: E Gibson, G Kingsley Ward;
   HMSO, 1989.
*Customs and Traditions of the Royal Air Force*:
   P G Hering; Gale and Polden, 1961.
*Knights of the Sky* - Parts 1 to 5:
   B R Holliss; Enthusiasts Publications,
   1985, 1986, 1988, 1989, 1992
*Lincolnshire Churches Revisited*: H Thorold;
   Michael Russell, 1989.
*Per Ardua Ad Astra, A Handbook of the Royal Air Force*: P Congdon; Airlife, 1987.
*The Unending Vigil, A History of the Commonwealth War Graves Commission 1917-1984*:
   P Longworth; Leo Cooper, 1985.
*War Memorials From Antiquity to the Present*:
   A Borg; Leo Cooper, 1991.
*Wings over Lincolnshire*:
   P H T Green, M Hodgson, W J Taylor;
   Midland Publishing, 1994.
*Wrecks & Relics*, 14th Edition: K Ellis;
   Midland Publishing, 1994.

## LATE ADDITIONS

The ever increasing number of memorials is reflected in this list of 'stop press' items. The OSGR is shown (where known) for those sites/locations which do not appear in the main text.

**BOTTESFORD (RAF/USAAF)**: Eucalyptus trees were planted on the site by former personnel of 463 and 467 Squadrons during May 1995, in memory of RAAF aircrew who lost their lives flying from the station. (See page 20)

**FISKERTON (RAF)**: A memorial stone to personnel from 49 and 576 Squadrons was dedicated on 21st May 1995. The memorial is at the side of one of the runways on an unclassified road which runs across the former airfield site itself, south of the A158, at OSGR 121/TF045732. (See also page 32)

**HARRINGTON**: On an unclassified road just off the A16 is a memorial stone to the crew of Lancaster III PB476 'PH-Y' of 12 Squadron, shot down in the early hours of 4th March 1945 by a Luftwaffe intruder. It was originally thought that the memorial was to be erected near to Harrington village but it is actually sited to the east, near Ulceby Cross. (See page 36)

**HEMSWELL (RAF)**: A memorial to all who served at RAF Hemswell from 1936-67, and especially those who lost their lives during the Second World War, is to be dedicated on 6th September 1995. (See page 36)

**KELSTERN**: During May 1995 the roll of honour of 625 Squadron was deposited in the village church (St Faith – 113/TF252899), which is on an unclassified road north of the A631. (See also page 37)

**LITTLE GRIMSBY**: In May 1995 a memorial plaque was dedicated in the village church (St Edith) to the crew of Lancaster I LL956 'CF-Q' of 625 Squadron, which crashed nearby on 14th October 1944. Little Grimsby is on an unclassified road east of the A16. (113/TF327913)

**RAUCEBY (RAF HOSPITAL)**: It is understood that a plaque was placed in Orchard House in May 1995, commemorating the hospital's role as an RAF hospital and its specialist burns unit. (See page 48)

**SPALDING**: A garden of remembrance, including an RAF section, is to be established at Ayscoughfee Gardens (131/TF251226) in the town centre. (See page 53)

**SPILSBY**: The roll of honour of 207 Squadron was presented to the people of Spilsby in May 1995. (122/TF400660)

**ULCEBY CROSS**: See Harrington.

**RAF WADDINGTON**: Former personnel of 463 and 467 Squadrons planted eucalyptus trees on the site during May 1995, in memory of RAAF aircrew who lost their lives flying from the station. Adjacent to the 8 Squadron crewroom is The Freddie West Room, commemorating Air Vice-Marshal F M F West vc and containing items relating to the unit's history. (See page 55)

## TOURIST INFORMATION

North Kesteven Tourism
Sleaford Tourist Information Centre
The Mill, Money's Yard, Carre Street, Sleaford
Lincolnshire, NG34 7TW
Tel: 01529 414294

West Lindsey Tourism Unit
West Lindsey District Council, The Guildhall
Gainsborough, Lincolnshire, DN21 2DH
Tel: 01427 615411 extension 254

Lincolnshire and South Humberside Tourism,
The Castle, Lincoln, LN1 3AA.
Tel: 01522 526450.

*Went the day well?*
*We died and never knew.*
*But well or ill,*
*for freedom, we died for you.*
ANON

# Other titles in this series from Midland Publishing

### BATTLE OF BRITAIN MEMORIAL FLIGHT
Bill Taylor

### CRANWELL RNAS & RAF PHOTOGRAPHS
Peter Green & Mike Hodgson

### WINGS OVER LINCOLNSHIRE
Peter Green, Mike Hodgson & Bill Taylor

Arguably the most stirring moment at any UK airshow is when the commentator announces that the Battle of Britain Memorial Flight are running in to display. Bill Taylor presents a loving pictorial salute to the Flight – not just as they appear today, but the entire history from the formative days at Biggin Hill in 1957 to the base at Coningsby and the visitor centre alongside.

A barrage of photographs, including a colour section showing the Flight in action, shows all aspects of the aircraft, displaying them and the ever-demanding task of keeping classic old aircraft in the air and in front of the eager public.

*Battle of Britain Memorial Flight* provides the first complete reference to the aircraft and the unit. As countless people get ready this year to marvel at the Flight and the meaning behind its aircraft, they now have a book that will give them the complete picture.

Cranwell in Lincolnshire has been associated with aeroplanes and aviation since late 1915. This book traces the story of the historical station using 130 photographs and extended captions, ranging from the early days of HMS Daedalus, RNAS right up to the present day.

The name Cranwell tends to be associated with the Royal Air Force College, but many other units have been based there during the airfield's lifetime.

The photographs are mainly from the College Library collection and in many cases have not previously been seen in print. These include scenes of the airfields construction, including the North and South airfields plus the Airship station. Also included are based aircraft, and some of the interesting visiting types, personalities of the times.

The contents of this book will invoke nostalgia amongst those many people who served at Cranwell, as well as providing useful information for historians. It will also appeal to visitors to the Cranwell Aviation Heritage Centre, situated one mile south-east of the airfield.

The rural county of Lincolnshire can perhaps lay claim to being England's premier aviation county. It is the home of the Royal Air Force College at Cranwell, and was host to thousands of Allied aircrew during the Second World War. The county's illustrious aviation heritage is now an attraction for many aviation enthusiasts and general tourists.

This new pictorial chronicles Lincolnshire's strong ties with the worlds of both civil and military aviation from before the First World War. The five sections begin with ballooning in the nineteenth century and continue through the First World War, the inter-war period, the Second World War and post-war to the present day Tornado and Sentry.

In addition to the aircraft, the personalities such as B C Hucks, Sir Alan Cobham and Alex Henshaw are included. The photographs come from local archives and private collections.

For the enthusiast, this is a fascinating gap-filler, and for the less committed, it is a useful introduction to Lincolnshire's diverse aviation history.

Softback
200 x 210 mm, 84 pages
116 b/w and 25 colour photographs
1 85780 028 1   Available
**£9.95**

Softback
200 x 210 mm, 48 pages
134 b/w and 3 colour photos
1 85780 014 1   Available
**£6.95**

Softback
200 x 210 mm, 48 pages
135 photos
1 85780 024 9   Available
**£7.95**

**We hope that you have enjoyed this book . . .**

Midland Publishing titles are carefully edited and designed for you by a knowledgeable and enthusiastic team of specialists, with many years experience.

Further titles are in the course of preparation but we would welcome ideas on what you would like to see. If you have a manuscript or project that requires publishing, we should be happy to consider it; but send only brief details initially, please.

In addition, our associate company, Midland Counties Publications, offers an exceptionally wide range of aviation, spaceflight, astronomy, military, naval and transport books and videos for sale by mail-order around the world.

For a copy of the appropriate catalogue, or to order further copies of this book, and any of the titles mentioned on this page, please write, telephone or fax to:

**Midland Counties Publications**
Unit 3 Maizefield,
Hinckley Fields
Hinckley, Leics
LE10 1YF

Tel: 01455 233 747   Fax: 01455 233 737